GEORGIAN COLLEGE LIBRARY 2582

250201
$79.00

D1309347

THE PORTABLE GUIDE
TO EVIDENCE

2nd Edition

by

Michael P. Doherty, B.A., M.A., LL.B.

Legal Counsel
Department of Justice

Library Commons
Georgian College
825 Memorial Avenue
Box 2316
Orillia, ON L3V 6S2

THOMSON
™
CARSWELL

© 2006 Thomson Canada Limited

All rights reserved. No part of this publication may be reproduced, stored in a retrieval system, or transmitted, in any form or by any means, electronic, mechanical, photocopying, recording, or otherwise, without the prior written permission of the publisher.

The publisher is not engaged in rendering legal, accounting or other professional advice. If legal advice or other expert assistance is required, the services of a competent professional should be sought. The analysis contained herein represents the opinions of the authors and should in no way be construed as being official or unofficial policy of any governmental body.

Library and Archives Canada Cataloguing in Publication

Doherty, Michael P. (Michael Patrick), 1957-
    The portable guide to evidence by Michael P. Doherty.-2nd ed.

Includes bibliographical references and index.
ISBN 0-459-24304-7

    1. Evidence (Law) — Canada. I. Title.

KE8440.D63 2006   347.71'06   C2006-900394-7
KF8935.ZA2D64 2006

Composition: Computer Composition of Canada Inc.

THOMSON
_{TM}
CARSWELL

One Corporate Plaza, 2075 Kennedy Road, Toronto, Ontario M1T 3V4
Customer Service:
Toronto 1-416-609-3800
Elsewhere in Canada/U.S. 1-800-387-5164
Fax 1-416-298-5094

PREFACE TO SECOND EDITION

When the first edition of this book was launched, it was in the belief that lawyers appearing in courts and before tribunals would find it useful to have an authoritative handbook that they could take with them for quick reference. Sales figures of the book suggest that lawyers did indeed perceive the benefit of such a volume. In addition, however, communications from tribunal chairs, law students and others have indicated that they have also found the book useful. This new edition is published in the hope of satisfying the continuing need of existing readers as well as attracting those who are now seeing the book for the first time.

In making revisions, every effort was made to conform to the three criteria that had guided the compilation of the first edition, namely that the book had to be small, easily referenced, and authoritative. The first of these three was the one to which it was most difficult to adhere, since it proved to be much easier to add new citations than to remove old ones; that said, the reader will not find the current edition much bigger than the previous one, and it should still slip easily into a trial bag.

The third criterion was the one that generated the most editorial debate, as to the appropriate balance between the authorial voice and the judicial quotations with which this book is liberally laced. As flattering as it would be to believe that courts would find my personal pronouncements on the law persuasive, I continue to believe that they are more likely to be convinced by the courts' own rulings on the law, particularly those of the Supreme Court of Canada. For that reason, wherever possible this book relies upon reported reasons for judgment to elucidate the law of evidence. Thanks are therefore due to all those judges whose words constitute so much of this volume.

As always, the editors at Carswell and I would be grateful for any suggestions as to changes or additions that could make future editions of the book even more useful.

Michael P. Doherty
Vancouver, B.C.
October 2005

FOREWORD

I write this Foreword a month after the author of this book, fifteen other counsel and I completed two and one-half years working together sorting out facts and responsibility with respect to the Asia Pacific Economic Cooperation Leaders' Meeting held on the University of British Columbia campus on November 25, 1997.

The phase of that exercise involving the presentation of viva voce evidence consumed 14 months of the work of the Commission of Inquiry. In asking that I prepare this foreword Mr. Doherty said:

> I originally conceived of the book while listening to some of the evidentiary arguments that arose before you in the APEC hearing. It seemed to me that even very capable counsel could sometimes become confused about basic points of evidence law, and that an easily referenced book that could refresh their memories might lead to a higher calibre of argument.

Having been called upon on scores of occasions during the course of the hearing to make rulings on contentious evidentiary matters, I can attest to the author's further view, expressed in the preface to the book, that evidentiary arguments most often arise unexpectedly with the result that counsel frequently have to scramble to speak to basic principles.

The author has done a great service to his colleague practitioners across the country in achieving his goal of preparing an easily referenced book that could refresh counsels' memory on almost the spur of the moment resulting in a higher calibre of an argument. For that latter result, those performing an adjudicative function will be equally grateful for the efforts of Mr. Doherty. Students of law will also find this to be a useful overview of the law on the intricate and changing subject of evidence.

The law on the issues that so often arise at trial, in both civil and criminal proceedings, is well organized and presented clearly and concisely. Of particular practical assistance is the generous reference to judicial quotes as authority for principles of law addressed in the book.

The objective in preparing this publication has certainly been achieved and its target audience will be well served by reference to it.

The Honourable E.N. (Ted) Hughes, Q.C.
Victoria, BC
September 2001

TABLE OF CONTENTS

TABLE OF CASES

1
IS IT EVIDENCE?

1. An Overview of the Law of Evidence

La Forest J. summed up the law of evidence as follows:[1]

> The organizing principles of the law of evidence may be simply stated. All relevant evidence is admissible, subject to a discretion to exclude matters that may unduly prejudice, mislead or confuse the trier of fact, take up too much time, or that should otherwise be excluded on clear grounds of law or policy. Questions of relevancy and exclusion are, of course, matters for the trial judge, but over the years many specific exclusionary rules have been developed for the guidance of the trial judge, so much so that the law of evidence may superficially appear to consist simply of a series of exceptions to the rules of admissibility, with exceptions to the exceptions, and their sub-exceptions.

The principle that there is a unified law of evidence, although it may differ in its application between civil and criminal matters, was noted by Lord Reading in *R. v. Christie*:[2]

> The principles of the laws of evidence are the same whether applied at civil or criminal trials, but they are not enforced with the same rigidity against a person accused of a criminal offence as against a party to a civil action.

2. Evidence Defined

In all of their deliberations on evidentiary matters, it is rare that courts have to answer the fundamental question "what is evidence". When they do, however, they are comfortable in adopting definitions from evidentiary texts. As Philp J.A. stated in *R. v. Zeolkowski:*[3]

> The word "evidence" has several meanings, but it is not an obscure or uncertain word. In *Phipson on Evidence*, 13th ed. (1982), para. 1-03, the author writes:

---

[1] *R. v. Corbett*, [1988] 1 S.C.R. 670 (S.C.C.) at 714, dissenting.

[2] [1914] A.C. 545 (U.K. H.L.) at 564, cited with approval in *Lewkowicz v. Korzewich* (1955), [1956] S.C.R. 170 (S.C.C.).

[3] (1987), 39 D.L.R. (4th) 45 (Man. C.A.) at 51, reversed (1989), 61 D.L.R. (4th) 725 (S.C.C.). The passage from *Phipson* was also adopted in, for example, *Saskatchewan (Attorney General) v. Saskatchewan (Provincial Court Judge)* (1994), 93 C.C.C. (3d) 483 (Sask. C.A.).

> Evidence, as used in judicial proceedings, has several meanings. The two main senses of the word are: first, the means, apart from argument and inference, whereby the court is informed as to the issues of fact as ascertained by the pleadings; secondly, the subject-matter of such means. The word is also used to denote that some fact may be admitted as proof and also in some cases that some fact has relevance to the issues of fact. In a real sense evidence is that which may be placed before the court in order that it may decide the issues of fact.

Another definition of evidence that has been accepted by Canadian courts[4] is in the introductory paragraph to *Cross on Evidence*:

> The evidence of a fact is that which tends to prove it – something which may satisfy an inquirer of the fact's existence.

In *Children's Aid Society of London & Middlesex v. M. (A.)*,[5] Campbell J. quoted *Black's* definition of evidence and then expounded as to the purpose of the law of evidence:[6]

> "Evidence" is defined *inter alia* in *Black's Law Dictionary*, 6th ed. (St. Paul, Minn.: West Publishing Co. 1990) as "that probative material, legally received, by which the tribunal may be lawfully persuaded of the truth or falsity of a fact in issue", and includes "all the means by which any alleged matter of fact, the truth of which is submitted to investigation, is established or disproved."

> The goals of the laws of evidence are to assist in the search for truth, to improve the efficiency of the trial process, to provide for the fairness of that trial process and to prevent the unfair bolstering of one party's evidence.

Finally, Proctor J.A. relied on *Blackstone's Commentaries*:[7]

> One of the clearest definitions of evidence is that in *Blackstone's Commentaries*, vol. III, p. 367: "Evidence signifies that which demonstrates, makes clear, or ascertains the truth of the very fact or point in issue, either on the one side or on the other."

Note, however, that the word "evidence" when used in a statute may mean something different from what would otherwise be legally

---

[4] See, *e.g.*, *R. v. Pfahler*, [1963] 2 C.C.C. 289 (Ont. C.A.) at 294; *Gould v. Yukon Order of Pioneers* (1991), 87 D.L.R. (4th) 618 (Y.T. S.C.) at 690, affirmed (1993), (sub nom. *Gould v. Yukon Order of Pioneers Dawson Lodge No. 1*) 100 D.L.R. (4th) 596 (Y.T. C.A.), leave to appeal allowed (1993), 82 B.C.L.R. (2d) xxxi (S.C.C.), affirmed (1996), 133 D.L.R. (4th) 449 (S.C.C.).

[5] (1998), [1998] O.J. No. 2530, 1998 CarswellOnt 3228 (Ont. Gen. Div.).

[6] *Ibid.*, at [CarswellOnt] paras. 13-14.

[7] *Sisters of Charity, Providence Hospital v. Saskatchewan (Labour Relations Board)*, [1951] 3 D.L.R. 735 (Sask. C.A.) at 754.

admissible evidence. A statutory provision that, for example, a court "may accept the evidence it considers proper" has been held to permit the court to receive as evidence material which, but for that provision, would be legally inadmissible.[8]

3. Testimony

Testimony is the form of evidence that for many people is synonymous with evidence itself.[9] The majority of evidence tendered is oral evidence, and many of the evidentiary rules that are discussed in this book were developed specifically for use with regard to oral evidence.

The importance of oral testimony was noted by Dickson C.J. in *R. v. Schwartz:*[10]

> One of the hallmarks of the common law of evidence is that it relies on witnesses as the means by which evidence is produced in court. As a general rule, nothing can be admitted as evidence before the court unless it is vouched for *viva voce* by a witness. Even real evidence, which exists independently of any statement by any witness, cannot be considered by the court unless a witness identifies it and establishes its connection to the events under consideration. Unlike other legal systems, the common law does not usually provide for self-authenticating documentary evidence.

It is not surprising therefore, that most rules of court make specific provision for oral testimony. Rule 40(2) of British Columbia's *Rules of Court*, for example, states:

> 40(2) Subject to any enactment and these rules,
>
> > (a) a witness at a trial of an action shall testify in open court, and
> > (b) unless the parties otherwise agree, the witness shall testify orally.

The various *Evidence Acts* also contain provisions dealing specifically with oral testimony, such as where a witness is unable to speak, where a witness is allowed to testify from behind a screen, or facilitating testimony of a witness ordered by a foreign tribunal.

---

[8] *Kelly v. Baker* (1996), [1996] B.C.J. No. 3050, 1996 CarswellBC 2156 (B.C. C.A.) at paras. 28-32.

[9] "In the circumstances of this appeal, it is sufficient to say that 'evidence' may be defined as the testimony of witnesses for the purpose of proving or disproving facts in legal proceedings." *R. v. Lavoie* (1970), 16 D.L.R. (3d) 647 (B.C. Co. Ct.) at 657, affirmed (1971), 23 D.L.R. (3d) 364 (B.C. C.A.). Quoted with approval in *R. v. McKay* (1971), 20 D.L.R. (3d) 336 (Man. C.A.) at 340.

[10] [1988] 2 S.C.R. 443 (S.C.C.) at 476, dissenting.

A definition of "testimony" was adopted by Steele J. in considering whether protection accorded to Ontario Labour Relations Board members against giving "testimony" protected them from discovery:[11]

> Testimony is defined in Jowitt's *Dictionary of English Law* as being "the evidence of a witness given *viva voce* in a court of justice or other tribunal".

4. Real Evidence

The nature of "real evidence" has assumed greater importance in the light of the *Canadian Charter of Rights and Freedoms*. In *R. v. Collins*,[12] Lamer J. in considering the use of a throat hold to forcibly obtain a condom containing heroin stated:[13]

> It is clear to me, that the factors relevant to this determination will include the nature of the evidence obtained as a result of the violation and the nature of the right violated and not so much the manner in which the right was violated. Real evidence that was obtained in a manner that violated the *Charter* will rarely operate unfairly for that reason alone. The real evidence existed irrespective of the violation of the *Charter* and its use does not render the trial unfair.

More recent cases suggest that the extent to which real evidence should trigger the operation of *Charter* provisions – *e.g.* s. 8 guarantees against unreasonable search and seizure – remains a live issue.[14]

As to the definition of "real evidence", in a case involving the use of an electronic tracking device, Cory J. for the majority noted:[15]

> Evidence has been found to be "real" when it referred to tangible items. For example narcotics were held to be real evidence in *R. v. Jacoy* (1988), 45 C.C.C. (3d) 46, [1988] 2 S.C.R. 548, 66 C.R. (3d) 336, and in *R. v. Debot* (1989), 52 C.C.C. (3d) 193, [1989] 2 S.C.R. 1140, 73 C.R. (3d) 129. Weapons were held to be real evidence in *R. v. Black* (1989), 50 C.C.C. (3d) 1, [1989] 2 S.C.R. 138, 70 C.R. (3d) 97. In all of these cases, the real or tangible evidence was admitted even though it had been obtained as a result of an unreasonable search.

---

[11] *Ellis-Don Ltd. v. Ontario (Labour Relations Board)* (1992), 95 D.L.R. (4th) 56 (Ont. Div. Ct.) at 61, reversed (1994), 110 D.L.R. (4th) 731 (Ont. Div. Ct.), leave to appeal refused (1994), 24 Admin. L.R. (2d) 122n (Ont. C.A.), leave to appeal refused (1995), 118 D.L.R. (4th) vi (note) (S.C.C.).

[12] [1987] 1 S.C.R. 265 (S.C.C.).

[13] *Ibid.*, at 284.

[14] *R. v. Buhay*, [2003] 1 S.C.R. 631 (S.C.C.) at para. 40.

[15] *R. v. Wise*, [1992] 1 S.C.R. 527 (S.C.C.) at 541.

A case involving a blood sample led Glube C.J.T.D.[16] to rely on a textbook definition of real evidence:[17]

> Whether a blood sample is a "thing" using a dictionary definition, or real evidence, that is, something which the court uses to make observations and draw conclusions from rather than relying on the testimony of a witness (Sopinka and Lederman, *The Law of Evidence in Civil Cases* (Butterworths, Toronto, 1974) at p. 12. . ..

A question on which there is divided jurisprudence is whether when a court takes a view – *i.e.* goes to look at the site of events in question – the view is a form of real evidence. Schultz J.A.,[18] relying on English Court of Appeal jurisprudence,[19] stated that a view taken by a tribunal is similar to an exhibit tendered as evidence:[20]

> I think it is a matter of everyday practice in our Courts that scale models, or similar objects, are tendered and accepted as real evidence. Such evidence may offer stronger and more convincing proof of the fact claimed than the oral evidence of witnesses. The Judge who views them in the court room is in no different position there than when, with all the necessary safeguards and conditions met, he views them outside the court room. When, as in the case of a road, it is impossible to bring the object into the court room and the trial Judge takes a proper view outside the court room, he is entitled to consider such a view as evidence. To hold otherwise seems to me unrealistic, for what better evidence could be offered to judges than what they can see with their own eyes? This is so whether the evidence is produced in Court or at the scene of an accident.

Ontario courts, on the other hand, have accepted that a view is not itself evidence, but is taken to better enable a court to understand the evidence.[21] Where, however, the purpose of taking a view goes beyond enabling the court to understand evidence and might be characterized as putting the judge in the shoes of an expert witness, then it may be objectionable.[22]

5. Documents

Documents are generally regarded as one of the major classifications of evidence. In considering them as evidence, it should first be

---

[16] *Glace Bay Community Hospital v. N.S.N.U.* (1992), 115 N.S.R. (2d) 120 (N.S. T.D.).
[17] *Ibid.*, at 127.
[18] *Meyers v. Manitoba* (1960), 26 D.L.R. (2d) 550 (Man. C.A.).
[19] *Buckingham v. Daily News Ltd.*, [1956] 2 All E.R. 904 (Eng. C.A.).
[20] *Supra*, note 18 at 558.
[21] See, for example, *Chambers v. Murphy*, [1953] 2 D.L.R. 705 (Ont. C.A.).
[22] *Adams v. Borrel* (2004), [2004] N.B.J. No. 298, 2004 CarswellNB 365 (N.B. Q.B.).

noted that many statutes, *Rules of Court* and *Evidence Act*s contain definitions of the term "document". Despite that, arguments have often occurred over questions such as whether an audio[23] or video[24] tape recording can be a "document".

The second point to note is that a document may be introduced into evidence either as, in effect, a piece of real evidence, where the purpose is simply to prove its existence rather than its contents; or may be introduced for the proof of its contents. Expressed another way, it may be introduced as evidence of the document's existence or evidence of the truth of its contents. If the latter, then it may be seen that *prima facie* it constitutes hearsay, and for this reason would not normally be admissible unless "proven" by a witness.

Estey J., in considering the use of a written prior inconsistent statement, quoted:[25]

> In Archbold, *Pleading, Evidence & Practice in Criminal Cases* (39th ed., 1976) at pp. 692-3 it is stated: It is submitted that the rule has been correctly formulated by Professor Cross: "Express or implied assertions of persons other than the witness who is testifying, and assertions in documents produced to the court when no witness is testifying are inadmissible as evidence of that which is asserted" (Cross, *Evidence* , 4th ed., p. 387) [underlining added].

Generally, the requirement for the admission of documents is as summed up by Dickson C.J. in *R. v. Schwartz:*[26]

> Before any document can be admitted into evidence there are two obstacles it must pass. First, it must be authenticated in some way by the party who wishes to rely on it. This authentication requires testimony by some witness; a document cannot simply be placed on the bench in front of the judge. Second, if the document is to be admitted as evidence of the truth of the statements it contains, it must be shown to fall within one of the exceptions to the hearsay rule. . ..

Note that some types of documents do not require such proof. See Chapter 3, "Is Proof Unnecessary?"

---

[23] See, for example, *Tide Shore Logging Ltd. v. Commonwealth Insurance Co.* (1979), 100 D.L.R. (3d) 112 (B.C. S.C.) and the cases considered therein.

[24] *Iannucci v. Heighton* (July 20, 1994), Doc. Vancouver B933591, [1994] B.C.J. No. 1721 (B.C. Master) at para. 7. The court held that the surveillance videotape was a "document".

[25] Concurring, *R. v. Rouse* (1978), (sub nom. *McInroy v. R.*) [1979] 1 S.C.R. 588 (S.C.C.) at 614.

[26] [1988] 2 S.C.R. 443 (S.C.C.) at 476.

6. "Scientific" Evidence

That novel scientific evidence is rarely discussed as a separate form of evidence is probably because it gets subsumed under the heading of expert opinion evidence. Arguably, however, while evidence of a novel scientific field may be adduced in order to form the basis for an expert opinion, it should be regarded as distinct from the opinion itself. Given that, the observations of Binnie J. in *R. v. J. (J-L.)*[27] are apposite:[28]

> *Mohan*[29] kept the door open to novel science, rejecting the "general acceptance" test formulated in the United States in *Frye v. United States*, 293 F. 1013 (D.C. Cir. 1923), and moving in parallel with its replacement, the "reliable foundation" test more recently laid down by the US Supreme Court in *Daubert v. Merrell Dow Pharmaceuticals, Inc.* 509 U.S. 579 (1993). While *Daubert* must be read in light of the specific text of the Federal Rules of Evidence, which differs from our own procedures, the U.S. Supreme Court did list a number of factors that could be helpful in evaluating the soundness of novel science (at pp. 593-94):
>
> (1) whether the theory or technique can be and has been tested:
>
> Scientific methodology today is based on generating hypotheses and testing them to see if they can be falsified; indeed, this methodology is what distinguishes science from other fields of human inquiry.
>
> (2) whether the theory or technique has been subjected to peer review and publication:
>
> [S]ubmission to the scrutiny of the scientific community is a component of "good science", in part because it increases the likelihood that substantive flaws in methodology will be detected.
>
> (3) the known or potential rate of error or the existence of standards; and,
>
> (4) whether the theory or technique used has been generally accepted:
>
> A "reliability assessment does not require, although it does permit, explicit identification of a relevant scientific community and an express determination of a particular degree of acceptance within that community."
>
> . . . . .

---

[27] (2000), 192 D.L.R. (4th) 416 (S.C.C.).
[28] *Ibid.*, at 430.
[29] *R. v. Mohan*, [1994] 2 S.C.R. 9 (S.C.C.).

Widespread acceptance can be an important factor in ruling particular evidence
admissible, and "a known technique which has been able to attract only minimal
support within the community," . . . may properly be viewed with skepticism.

When considering evidence in a comprehensive way, it is important to remember one central precept, namely that courts cannot make
their decisions in a vacuum, relying solely on abstract principles. They
must rely upon evidence — whatever its form — that counsel brings
before them. As will be seen in succeeding chapters, a state of dynamic
tension is created by the need for counsel to adduce argument and the
need for courts to ensure that the evidence is sufficiently reliable to form
the basis for their decisions.

2
CAN IT BE ADDUCED?

While some witnesses may possess relevant evidence, they may be unable or unwilling to testify.

1. Competency

The common law prohibited spouses, parties to civil litigation, and the defendants in criminal cases from giving evidence until the mid-nineteenth century, when a series of statutory reforms removed these obstacles to competency. Issues of competency still arise, however, in the case of spouses, children, the mentally impaired, and those who are part of the court system, such as judges, jurors and lawyers.

(a) Spouses

The law regarding spousal incompetence was stated by Lamer C.J. and Iacobucci J. for the majority in *R. v. Hawkins*:[1]

> The common law rule is that a spouse is an incompetent witness in criminal proceedings in which the other spouse is an accused, except where the charge involves the person, liberty or health of the witness spouse. See, e.g., *Lord Audley's Case* (1631), Hutt. 115, 123 E.R. 1140, at p. 1141; *Bentley v. Cooke* (1784), 3 Doug. K.B. 422, 99 E.R. 729; *R. v. Bissell* (1882), 1 O.R. 514 (Q.B.). The traditional rule has been modified by the passage of the *Canada Evidence Act*. Section 4(1) of the Act makes a spouse competent to testify on behalf of the accused in a criminal trial, and s. 4(2) makes the spouse both competent and compellable for the Crown for certain specified offences which generally tend to implicate the health and security of the witness spouse. But these statutory exceptions aside, the Act otherwise preserves the general common law rule that the spouse of an accused, willing or not, is not competent to testify against the accused at the behest of the Crown.
>
> At common law, it was well accepted that the rule of spousal incompetency renders a spouse incapable of testifying in relation to events which occurred both before and during the marriage: *Pedley v. Wellesley* (1829), 3 C. & P. 558, 172 E.R. 545. See Wigmore on Evidence (McNaughton rev. 1961), vol. 8, at sec.

---

[1] [1996] 3 S.C.R. 1043 (S.C.C.) at 1068-9.

2230. This principle was more recently underscored by the Alberta Court of Appeal in *R. v. Lonsdale* (1973), 15 C.C.C. (2d) 201. Citing common law authorities continued under s. 4(5) of the *Canada Evidence Act*, Sinclair J.A. held for the Court of Appeal, at p. 203, that the Crown may not call the spouse of an accused as a competent witness to testify in relation to events which occurred prior to the marriage.

Section 4 of the *Canada Evidence Act*, referred to by the Court, currently reads as follows:

Accused and Spouse
4. (1) Every person charged with an offence, and, except as otherwise provided in this section, the wife or husband, as the case may be, of the person so charged, is a competent witness for the defence, whether the person so charged is charged solely or jointly with any other person.

Accused and spouse
(2) The wife or husband of a person charged with an offence under subsection 136(1) of the *Youth Criminal Justice Act* or with an offence under any of sections 151, 152, 153, 155 or 159, subsection 160(2) or (3), or sections 170 to 173, 179, 212, 215, 218, 271 to 273, 280 to 283, 291 to 294 or 329 of the *Criminal Code*, or an attempt to commit any such offence, is a competent and compellable witness for the prosecution without the consent of the person charged.

Communications during marriage
(3) No husband is compellable to disclose any communication made to him by his wife during their marriage, and no wife is compellable to disclose any communication made to her by her husband during their marriage.

Offences against young persons
(4) The wife or husband of a person charged with an offence against any of sections 220, 221, 235, 236, 237, 239, 240, 266, 267, 268 or 269 of the *Criminal Code* where the complainant or victim is under the age of fourteen years is a competent and compellable witness for the prosecution without the consent of the person charged.

Saving
(5) Nothing in this section affects a case where the wife or husband of a person charged with an offence may at common law be called as a witness without the consent of that person.

Failure to testify
(6) The failure of the person charged, or of the wife or husband of that person, to testify shall not be made the subject of comment by the judge or by counsel for the prosecution.

The majority of the court in *Hawkins* held that any significant change to the rule should not be made by the courts, but should rather be left to Parliament.

An exception to the rule for spouses who are separated without any reasonable possibility of reconciliation was established by the Court in *R. v. Salituro*.[2]

Criticisms of the rule against spousal competence are noted by the Supreme Court of Canada in its judgments. One manifestation of judicial dissatisfaction was the decision of McIsaac J. in *R. v. Edelenbos*,[3] which held that:

> ...the common-law rule of spousal incompetency which is limited to unions recognized by provincial law involving wives and husbands offends s.15(1) of the *Charter of Rights and Freedoms* . It is hereby declared to be of no force and effect pursuant to s.52(1) of the *Constitution Act, 1982* .

On the basis of that ruling, it was found that a common law spouse was competent to testify against her accused partner.

(b) Children and the Mentally Impaired

Sections 16 and 16.1 of the *Canada Evidence Act* deal with the capacity of children and the mentally impaired to give evidence:

Witness whose capacity is in question
16. (1) If a proposed witness is a person of fourteen years of age or older whose mental capacity is challenged, the court shall, before permitting the person to give evidence, conduct an inquiry to determine

> (a) whether the person understands the nature of an oath or a solemn affirmation; and
> (b) whether the person is able to communicate the evidence.

Testimony under oath or solemn affirmation
(2) A person referred to in subsection (1) who understands the nature of an oath or a solemn affirmation and is able to communicate the evidence shall testify under oath or solemn affirmation.

Testimony on promise to tell truth
(3) A person referred to in subsection (1) who does not understand the nature of an oath or a solemn affirmation but is able to communicate the evidence may,

---

[2] [1991] 3 S.C.R. 654 (S.C.C.).
[3] (2000), [2000] O.J. No. 2147, 2000 CarswellOnt 2014 (Ont. S.C.J.).

notwithstanding any provision of any Act requiring an oath or a solemn affirmation, testify on promising to tell the truth.

Inability to testify
(4) A person referred to in subsection (1) who neither understands the nature of an oath or a solemn affirmation nor is able to communicate the evidence shall not testify.

Burden as to capacity of witness
(5) A party who challenges the mental capacity of a proposed witness of fourteen years of age or more has the burden of satisfying the court that there is an issue as to the capacity of the proposed witness to testify under an oath or a solemn affirmation.

Person under fourteen years of age
16.1 (1) A person under fourteen years of age is presumed to have the capacity to testify.

No oath or solemn affirmation
(2) A proposed witness under fourteen years of age shall not take an oath or make a solemn affirmation despite a provision of any Act that requires an oath or a solemn affirmation.

Evidence shall be received
(3) The evidence of a proposed witness under fourteen years of age shall be received if they are able to understand and respond to questions.

Burden as to capacity of witness
(4) A party who challenges the capacity of a proposed witness under fourteen years of age has the burden of satisfying the court that there is an issue as to the capacity of the proposed witness to understand and respond to questions.

Court inquiry
(5) If the court is satisfied that there is an issue as to the capacity of a proposed witness under fourteen years of age to understand and respond to questions, it shall, before permitting them to give evidence, conduct an inquiry to determine whether they are able to understand and respond to questions.

Promise to tell truth
(6) The court shall, before permitting a proposed witness under fourteen years of age to give evidence, require them to promise to tell the truth.

Understanding of promise
(7) No proposed witness under fourteen years of age shall be asked any questions regarding their understanding of the nature of the promise to tell the truth for the purpose of determining whether their evidence shall be received by the court.

Effect

(8) For greater certainty, if the evidence of a witness under fourteen years of age is received by the court, it shall have the same effect as if it were taken under oath.

The nature of the "inquiry" the court is to make under s. 16(1) was considered in *R. v. Marquard*.[4] McLachlin J. for the majority made the following observations:[5]

> In the case of a child testifying under s. 16 of the *Canada Evidence Act* testimonial competence is not presumed. The child is placed in the same position as an adult whose competence has been challenged. At common law, such a challenge required the judge to inquire into the competence of the witness to testify.
>
> Testimonial competence comprehends: (1) the capacity to observe (including interpretation); (2) the capacity to recollect; and (3) the capacity to communicate: *McCormick on Evidence* (4th ed. 1992), vol. 1, at pp. 242-48; *Wigmore on Evidence* (Chadbourn revision 1979), vol. 2, at pp. 636-38. The judge must satisfy him- or herself that the witness possesses these capacities. Is the witness capable of observing what was happening? Is he or she capable of remembering what he or she observes? Can he or she communicate what he or she remembers? The goal is not to ensure that the evidence is credible, but only to assure that it meets the minimum threshold of being receivable. The enquiry is into capacity to perceive, recollect and communicate, not whether the witness actually perceived, recollects and can communicate about the events in question. Generally speaking, the best gauge of capacity is the witness's performance at the time of trial. The procedure at common law has generally been to allow a witness who demonstrates capacity to testify at trial to testify. Defects in ability to perceive or recollect the particular events at issue are left to be explored in the course of giving the evidence, notably by cross-examination.
>
> I see no indication in the wording of s. 16 that Parliament intended to revise this time-honoured process. The phrase "communicate the evidence" indicates more than mere verbal ability. The reference to "the evidence" indicates the ability to testify about the matters before the court. It is necessary to explore in a general way whether the witness is capable of perceiving events, remembering events and communicating events to the court. If satisfied that this is the case, the judge may then receive the child's evidence, upon the child's promising to tell the truth under s. 16(3). It is not necessary to determine in advance that the child perceived and recollects the very events at issue in the trial as a condition of ruling that the child's evidence be received. That is not required of adult witnesses, and should not be required for children.

---

[4] [1993] 4 S.C.R. 223 (S.C.C.).

[5] *Ibid.*, at 236.

(c) Judges, Jurors and Lawyers

Categories of individuals who are neither competent nor compellable to testify because of their roles in the judicial process were summed up by Cameron J. in *Koita v. Toronto Police Services Board*,[6] in a decision establishing that justices of the peace are immune from litigation:[7]

> A member of an administrative tribunal must be independent and is neither compellable or competent to testify as to the tribunal's proceedings: *Ermina v. Canada (Minister of Citizenship and Immigration)*, [1998] F.C.J. No. 1785 citing in support *MacKeigan v. Hickman* (1988), 43 C.C.C. (3d) 287 (N.S.T.D.) (affirmed [1989] 2 S.C.R. 797) which established that a judge is neither competent nor compellable to testify respecting his or her adjudicative functions. See also *Taylor v. Canada (Attorney General)*, [1997] F.C.J. No. 1748 deciding that a justice is neither compellable nor competent to testify. Jurors have the same immunity as a judge and are neither compellable nor competent to testify before an inquiry into a wrongful conviction: *Re Morin* (1997), 154 D.LR. (4th) 146.

2. Compellability

Generally speaking, if someone is not competent, it must logically follow that they are not compellable. This is generally the case, for example, with judges, juries and lawyers, and with the spouse of an accused. Persons who are competent, on the other hand, are normally compellable. Notable exceptions are any sovereigns or heads of foreign states, who are immune from the jurisdiction of any court in Canada.[8]

The right of the accused to be secure against self-incrimination does not only involve the question of compellability in the trial of the accused. It can also involve testimony given in other proceedings, and the use of that testimony in a subsequent trial. This was the case in *R. v. Noël*,[9] in which Arbour J. for the majority summed up the rule:[10]

> When an accused testifies at trial, he cannot be cross-examined on the basis of a prior testimony unless the trial judge is satisfied that there is no realistic danger that his prior testimony could be used to incriminate him. The danger of incrim-

---

[6] (2000), [2000] O.J. No. 4785, 2000 CarswellOnt 4826 (Ont. S.C.J.), reversed on other grounds (2001), 151 O.A.C. 360 (Ont. Div. Ct.).

[7] *Ibid.*, at [2000] para 24.

[8] *State Immunity Act*, R.S.C. 1985, c. S-18, ss. 1 and 3.

[9] [2002] 3 S.C.R. 433 (S.C.C.).

[10] *Ibid.*, at 441.

ination will vary with the nature of the prior evidence and the circumstances of the case including the efficacy of an adequate instruction to the jury.

(a) The Accused in a Criminal Prosecution

The right of an accused to silence at trial is well known and is not in itself generally controversial. The interpretation that can be placed upon the exercise of the right to silence, however, whether in the court-room or outside of it, is an issue that continues to arise. That is, if an accused exercises the fundamental right to silence, can the exercise of that right be argued to be evidence of guilt? If it could, that would obviously greatly undermine the value of the right to silence. The courts, however, have frequently had to deal with assertions by the Crown that silence can be indicative of guilt.

In *R. v. Turcotte*,[11] for example, the accused had walked into a police station and repeatedly asked the police to drive to the ranch where he lived, without telling them why he was asking or what they would find there. When they did so, they found three people who had been attacked with an axe, all of whom died. At trial, the judge told the jury that the refusal of the accused to respond to police questions was "post-offence conduct" and that an inference of guilt could be drawn from it. A jury convicted the accused, but the conviction was set aside on appeal. Abella J. for the Supreme Court of Canada reviewed the general principle of the right to silence:[12]

> Under the traditional common law rules, absent statutory compulsion, everyone has the right to be silent in the face of police questioning. This right to refuse to provide information or answer inquiries finds cogent and defining expression in *Rothman v. The Queen*, [1981] 1 S.C.R. 640, *per* Lamer J.:
>
> > In Canada the right of a suspect not to say anything to the police . . . is merely the exercise by him of the general right enjoyed in this country by anyone to do whatever one pleases, saying what one pleases or choosing not to say certain things, unless obliged to do otherwise by law. It is because no law says that a suspect, save in certain circumstances, must say anything to the police that we say that he has the right to remain silent, which is a positive way of explaining that there is on his part no legal obligation to do otherwise. [Footnotes omitted; p. 683]

While noting that the "temporal limits" of the right to silence have not yet been fully defined, Abella J. also noted that the right to silence

---

[11] 2005 SCC 50 (S.C.C.).

[12] *Ibid.*, at para 41.

had received *Charter* benediction in *R. v. Hebert*.[13] In that case, Mc-Lachlin J. had founded the s. 7 right to silence in two common law doctrines: the confessions rule and the privilege against self-incrimination, explaining that both emerge from the following unifying theme:[14]

> [T]he idea that a person in the power of the state in the course of the criminal process has the right to choose whether to speak to the police or remain silent.

Abella J. did, however, also note the exceptions to the right to silence, quoting Cory J in *R. v. Chambers*[15] that if "the Crown can establish a real relevance and a proper basis", evidence of silence can be admitted with an appropriate warning to the jury. Examples cited included *R. v. Crawford*,[16] where one of two co-accused was cross-examined about his failure to make a statement to police by counsel for the other; this was held to be permissible as long as it was only used to assess credibility, not to infer guilt. It was noted that evidence of silence may also be admissible when the defence raises an issue that renders the silence of the accused relevant, such as the accused's cooperation with the authorities (*R. v. Lavallee*),[17] testimony by the accused that he had denied the charges against him at the time he was arrested (*R. v. O. (G.A.)*),[18] or where silence was relevant to a defence theory of mistaken identity and a flawed police investigation (*R. v. W. (M.C.)*).[19] Another exception noted was where the accused failed to disclose his or her alibi in a timely or adequate manner: *R. v. Cleghorn*.[20] Silence might also be admissible if it is inextricably bound up with the narrative or other evidence and cannot easily be extricated.

The judgment in *Turcotte* also made it very clear that the right to silence exists at all times, including times when a person has not been arrested or detained, and that it is not waived simply because a person voluntarily chooses to make *some* communication with the police.

---

[13] [1990] 2 S.C.R. 151 (S.C.C.).
[14] *Ibid.*, at para 78.
[15] [1990] 2 S.C.R. 1293 (S.C.C.).
[16] [1995] 1 S.C.R. 858 (S.C.C.).
[17] (January 31, 1980), MacKinnon A.C.J.O., Martin J.A., Zuber J.A., [1980] O.J. No. 540 (Ont. C.A.).
[18] (1997), 200 A.R. 363 (Alta. C.A.).
[19] 169 B.C.A.C. 128, 2002 BCCA 341 (B.C. C.A.).
[20] [1995] 3 S.C.R. 175 (S.C.C.).

(b) Compellability Under s. 83.28 of the *Criminal Code* (Terrorism)

The notion of compellability in the courts was dramatically affected by the passage of s. 83.28 of the *Criminal Code*, which permits a peace officer acting with the authorization of the Attorney General to apply to a judge for an order for the "gathering of information" where there are reasonable grounds to believe that a terrorism offence has been committed. Such an order compels a person named in the order to appear before a judge for examination by an agent of the Attorney General. The person being examined is not excused from answering questions on the grounds of self incrimination, but answers and evidence derived from their examination are not to be used against them in criminal proceedings, other than those for perjury or giving contradictory evidence.

A majority of the Supreme Court has held that s. 83.28 is not unconstitutional, with only a dissenting minority finding that it unduly compromises judicial independence and impartiality.[21] The variety of judgments handed down by the Court in that instance illustrate, however, the difficulties that courts will face if they are forced to continue to balance the use of this powerful investigative tool against the values of a free and democratic society.

(c) The Spouse of an Accused in a Criminal Prosecution

As discussed above, the spouse of an accused was not competent at common law. It logically follows that the spouse of an accused also must not be compellable at common law. The question arises of whether in those cases where an exception to the rule makes one spouse competent to testify against the other, the spouse also becomes compellable.

In *R. v. McGinty*,[22] McLachlin J.A. (as she then was) for the majority noted that no pre-twentieth century common law cases had determined the question, but that:[23]

> While there are no cases holding that a spouse is a compellable witness against his or her spouse in cases involving violence by the charged spouse against the witness-spouse, there exists at common law a general principle which is of assis-

---

[21] *Application Under s. 83.28 of the Criminal Code, Re*, [2004] 2 S.C.R. 248 (S.C.C.).

[22] [1986] 4 W.W.R. 97 (Y.T. C.A.).

[23] *Ibid.*, at 113.

tance in solving the question of what the common law on the subject was. That is the long-recognized and fundamental principle that a competent witness is a compellable witness. A person who is a competent witness and who has material evidence on a case can be compelled, subject to the protection of privilege on specific questions, to attend in court and testify.

McLachlin J.A.'s conclusion was that:[24]

On the basis of the authorities and policy, I conclude that the trial judge was correct in ruling that under s. 4(4) of the *Canada Evidence Act* spouses are competent and compellable witnesses against their spouses in cases involving violence against them.

Two other judgments of provincial courts of appeal which arrived at the same conclusion were cited in the concurring judgment of Lambert J.A.: *R. v. Sillars* (1979), 45 C.C.C. (2d) 283 (B.C. C.A.); and *R. v. Lonsdale* (1973), 15 C.C.C. (2d) 201 (Alta. C.A.).

(d) Complainants in Sexual Assault Prosecutions

A statutory exemption from compellability is given to the complainant in sexual assault cases on the *voir dire* that may be held to determine why the accused should be allowed to adduce evidence of the complainant's sexual history. The constitutionality of this provision was upheld in *R. v. Darrach*,[25] as per Gonthier J.:[26]

The complainant is not compellable at the *voir dire* pursuant to s. 276.2(2). This provision is both constitutional and an important aspect of s. 276. The accused argues that he is *de facto* compellable *because* the complainant is non-compellable at the *voir dire*. I have already established that he is not compellable nor being compelled at law. His desire to have the complainant testify flows, as would his need to testify himself, from his tactical decision to present evidence and the ensuing need to show its relevance. As we have seen, there is no legal compulsion nor violation of the accused's constitutional rights. Furthermore, the complainant's **non-compellability** is based on sound legislative goals. To compel the complainant to be examined on her sexual history before the subject has been found to be relevant to the trial would defeat two of the three purposes of the law, as articulated and upheld in *Seaboyer* (at p. 606). It is an invasion of the complainant's privacy and discourages the reporting of crimes of sexual violence. As the Ontario Court of Appeal points out, the accused must know what evidence he wants to introduce on his own; the *voir dire* is not to be a "fishing expedition"

---

[24] *Ibid.* at 122.

[25] [2000] S.C.J. No. 46, 2000 CarswellOnt 3321, 2000 CarswellOnt 3322 (S.C.C.).

[26] *Ibid.*, at paras. 68-9.

(p. 21). The evidence is tested at the *voir dire* and if it meets the criteria in s. 276(2), it may be introduced at trial. The complainant can then be compelled to testify or if the Crown, as it is most likely to do, calls her as a witness, be cross-examined on it.

The right to make full answer and defence, moreover, does not provide a right to cross-examine an accuser. This was explicitly held in *R. v. Cook*, [1997] 1 S.C.R. 1113, where the Court affirmed the broad discretion of the Crown to conduct its case. The Crown is free from any requirement to call particular witnesses, and this applies even to the victim of the crime for which the accused faces conviction (at para. 19).

It can be seen that issues of competence and compellability have been shaped at least as much by societal values as by any concerns about reliability. As societal attitudes toward the family and toward the rights of children, the mentally handicapped and others continue to evolve, it seems likely that the judicial approach to competence and compellability will also continue to do so.

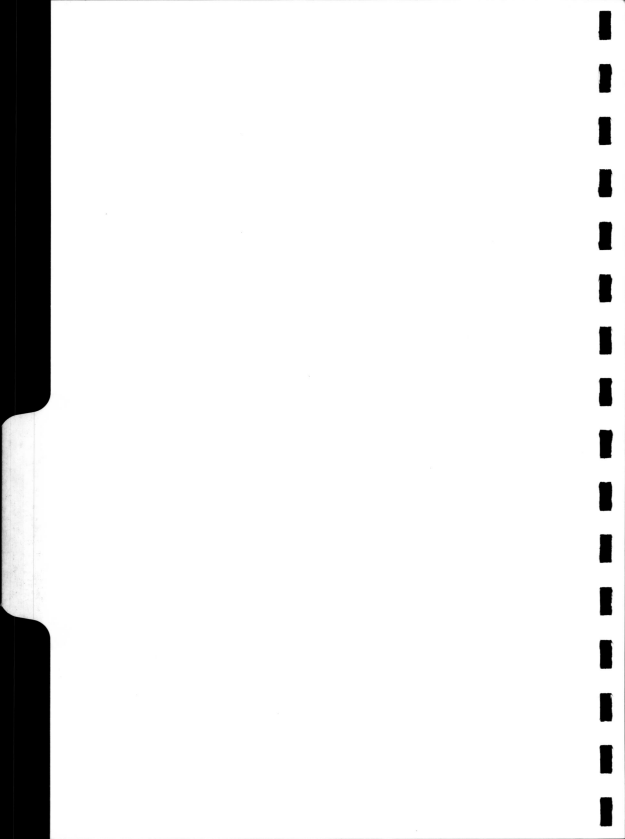

3

IS PROOF UNNECESSARY?

While the law of evidence is concerned with proving facts in court, it is not necessary to prove every fact. Some may be accepted as the result of legal principles while others are facts so familiar or universally recognized as to be unquestionable.

1. Presumptions

Pigeon J. in *R. v. Proudlock*[1] gives an explanation of presumptions:[2]

In the *Dictionary of English Law* by Earl Jowitt one reads:

> *Prima facie* evidence, that which, not being inconsistent with the falsity of the hypothesis, nevertheless raises such a degree of probability in its favour that it must prevail if believed by the jury unless rebutted or the contrary proved; conclusive evidence, on the other hand, is that which excludes or at least tends to exclude, the possibility of the truth of any other hypothesis than the one attempted to be established.

In *Tremblay v. The Queen* [[1969] S.C.R. 431.], this Court dealing with the presumption of fact arising out of the possession of recently stolen goods, adopted as a correct statement of its burden on the accused the following statement from *Phipson on Evidence* (10th ed. p. 53):

> On charges of stealing or receiving, proof of recent possession of the stolen property by the accused, if unexplained or not reasonably explained, or if, though reasonably explained, the explanation is disbelieved, raises a presumption of fact, though not of law, that he is the thief or receiver according to the circumstances; and upon such unexplained, or not reasonably explained, possession, or disbelieved explanation, the jury may (though not must) find him guilty. It is not, however, for the accused to prove honest dealing with the property, but for the prosecution to prove the reverse; and if any explanation be given which the jury think may be true, though they are not convinced that it is, they must acquit, for the main burden of proof (i.e. that of establishing guilt beyond reasonable doubt) rests throughout upon the prosecution, and in this case will not have been discharged.

---

[1] (1978), [1979] 1 S.C.R. 525 (S.C.C.).
[2] *Ibid.*, at 548-51.

In my view there should be no difference between the effect of a presumption of fact and of a presumption of law which is not expressed in such terms as to require the accused to "establish" or to "prove" a given fact or excuse as in subs. 237(1)(a) or subs. 247(3). When a presumption of law is expressed in such terms, it is settled that the burden on the accused is to prove the fact or excuse on the preponderance of evidence or on a balance of probabilities.

Such is not the situation when all the presumption does is to establish a *prima facie* case. The burden of proof does not shift. The accused does not have to "establish" a defence or an excuse, all he has to do is to raise a reasonable doubt. If there is nothing in the evidence adduced by the Crown from which a reasonable doubt can arise, then the accused will necessarily have the burden of adducing evidence if he is to escape conviction. However, he will not have the burden of proving his innocence, it will be sufficient if, at the conclusion of the case on both sides, the trier of fact has a reasonable doubt. In reasons endorsed by a majority of the Court in *The Queen v. Newton* [[1977] 1 S.C.R. 399.], at p. 411, the following passage from the judgment of the English Court of Criminal Appeal in *R. v. Spurge* [[1961] 2 Q.B. 205.], at p. 212, a dangerous driving case, was quoted with approval:

> It has been argued by counsel for the Crown that even if a mechanical defect can operate as defence, yet the onus of establishing this defence is upon the accused. It is of course conceded by the Crown that this onus is discharged if the defence is made out on a balance of probabilities. In the opinion of this court, the contention made on behalf of the Crown is unsound, for in cases of dangerous driving the onus never shifts to the defence. This does not mean that if the Crown proves that a motor-car driven by the accused has endangered the public, the accused could successfully submit at the end of the case for the prosecution that he had no case to answer on the ground that the Crown had not negatived the defence of mechanical defect. The court will consider no such special defence unless and until it is put forward by the accused. Once, however, it has been put forward it must be considered with the rest of the evidence in the case. If the accused's explanation leaves a real doubt in the mind of the jury, then the accused is entitled to be acquitted. If the jury rejects the accused's explanation, the jury should convict.

I can see no reason for applying a different test when the presumption against the accused is enacted by Parliament instead of being some presumption of fact applicable in situations which are all pretty well defined by a long series of cases, such as the presumptions arising out of possession of recently stolen goods or dangerous driving. Otherwise, it would mean that Parliament cannot make such presumptions statutory without altering them.

In my view, there are in our criminal law only three standards of evidence:

1. Proof beyond a reasonable doubt which is the standard to be met by the Crown against the accused;

2. Proof on a preponderance of the evidence or a balance of probabilities which is the burden of proof on the accused when he has to meet a presumption requiring him to establish or to prove a fact or an excuse;

3. Evidence raising a reasonable doubt which is what is required to overcome any other presumption of fact or of law.

Although I strongly believe in adhering to literal construction and in giving effect to every word of an enactment, I cannot find any substantial difference between "evidence to the contrary" and "any evidence to the contrary". Both expressions are equally the converse of "no evidence to the contrary" and there is no basis for a distinction depending on the presence or absence of the word "any". It is important to avoid unnecessary complexities and subtleties in the law of evidence by undue emphasis on minor differences in the wording of enactments. It would be especially unfortunate if this was the result of amendments intended to replace two technical Latin words by plain English or French words.

In *Batary v. Attorney General of Saskatchewan* [[1965] S.C.R. 465.], at p. 476, Cartwright J., as he then was, said speaking for the Court:

> If I am right in the view, which I have already expressed, that in 1870 the accused would not have been a compellable witness at such an inquest, it would, in my opinion, require clear words to bring about so complete a change in the law.

The standard of evidence required for a conviction, including the standard of the evidence required to overcome a *prima facie* case against the accused, is just as basic a principle as the right of the accused to remain silent. In fact, it may be considered as a qualification of this principle. The accused may remain silent but, when there is a *prima facie* case against him and he is, as in the instant case, the only person who can give "evidence to the contrary" his choice really is to face certain conviction or to offer in testimony whatever explanation or excuse may be available to him.

If the *prima facie* case is made up by the proof of facts from which guilt may be inferred by presumption of fact, the law is clear on the authorities that, because the case in the end must be proved beyond a reasonable doubt, it is not necessary for the accused to establish his innocence, but only to raise a reasonable doubt. This he may do by giving evidence of an explanation that may reasonably be true, and it will be sufficient unless he is disbelieved by the trier of fact, in which case his testimony is no evidence. In any case, the evidence given by himself or otherwise, has to be such as will at least raise a reasonable doubt as to his guilt; if it does not meet this test the *prima facie* case remains and conviction will ensue.

Dickson C.J. in the *Charter* case of *R. v. Oakes*,[3] which dealt with the provision in s. 8 of the *Narcotic Control Act* that makes possession of a narcotic presumptively for the purpose of trafficking, gave the following classification of presumptions:[4]

> In determining the meaning of these words, it is helpful to consider in a general sense the nature of presumptions. Presumptions can be classified into two general categories: presumptions without basic facts and presumptions with basic facts. A presumption without a basic fact is simply a conclusion which is to be drawn until the contrary is proved. A presumption with a basic fact entails a conclusion to be drawn upon proof of the basic fact (see *Cross On Evidence*, 5th ed., at pp. 122-23).
>
> Basic fact presumptions can be further categorized into permissive and mandatory presumptions. A permissive presumption leaves it optional as to whether the inference of the presumed fact is drawn following proof of the basic fact. A mandatory presumption requires that the inference be made.
>
> Presumptions may also be either rebuttable or irrebuttable. If a presumption is rebuttable, there are three potential ways the presumed fact can be rebutted. First, the accused may be required merely to raise a reasonable doubt as to its existence. Secondly, the accused may have an evidentiary burden to adduce sufficient evidence to bring into question the truth of the presumed fact. Thirdly, the accused may have a legal or persuasive burden to prove on a balance of probabilities the non-existence of the presumed fact.
>
> Finally, presumptions are often referred to as either presumptions of law or presumptions of fact. The latter entail "frequently recurring examples of circumstantial evidence" (*Cross on Evidence*, supra, at p. 124) while the former involve actual legal rules.

Cory J. for the majority in *R. v. Downey*[5] cited the above passage and added the following:[6]

> A very useful analysis of presumptions that can be utilized in this case can be found in the writing of T. A. Cromwell in "Proving Guilt: The Presumption of Innocence and the *Canadian Charter of Rights and Freedoms*", in W. H. Charles, T. A. Cromwell and K. B. Jobson, eds., *Evidence and the Charter of Rights and Freedoms* (1989), 125, at pp. 130ff. (which in turn is based on the analysis favoured by Professor Cross in *Evidence* (5th ed. 1979), at pp. 122ff., approved in *Oakes*). The presumptions can be summarized in this way:

---

[3] [1986] 1 S.C.R. 103 (S.C.C.).

[4] *Ibid.*, at 115-6.

[5] [1992] 2 S.C.R. 10 (S.C.C.).

[6] *Ibid.*, at 22.

(1) Presumptions which operate without the requirement of proof of any basic facts.

(2) Presumptions which require proof of a basic fact.

(a) Permissive Inferences: Where the trier of fact is entitled to infer a presumed fact from the proof of the basic fact, but is not obliged to do so. This results in a tactical burden whereby the accused may wish to call evidence in rebuttal, but is not required to do so.

(b) Evidential Burdens: Where the trier of fact is required to draw the conclusion from proof of the basic fact in the absence of evidence to the contrary. This mandatory conclusion results in an evidential burden whereby the accused will need to call evidence, unless there is already evidence to the contrary in the Crown's case.

(c) Legal Burdens: Similar to the burden in (b) except that the presumed fact must be disproved on a balance of probabilities instead of by the mere raising of evidence to the contrary. These are also referred to as "reverse onus clauses".

2. Judicial Notice

(a) When Can Judicial Notice be Taken?

The doctrine of judicial notice was considered by the Supreme Court of Canada in *R. v. Krymowski*,[7] a case in which the trial judge had wrongly refused to take notice of the fact that "Roma" and "gypsy" are synonymous, despite the Crown having proffered dictionary definitions that indicated this was the case. Charron J. said:[8]

> A court may accept without the requirement of proof facts that are either "(1) so notorious or generally accepted as not to be the subject of debate among reasonable persons; or (2) capable of immediate and accurate demonstration by resort to readily accessible sources of indisputable accuracy": *R. v. Find*, [2001] 1 S.C.R. 863, 2001 SCC 32, at para. 48. The dictionary meaning of words may fall within the latter category: see J. Sopinka, S. N. Lederman and A. W. Bryant, *The Law of Evidence in Canada* (2nd ed. 1999), at paras. 9.13 and 19.22.

The underlying rationale for the doctrine had previously been considered by L'Heureux-Dubé J. in *Moge v. Moge*:[9]

---

[7] [2005] 1 S.C.R. 101 (S.C.C.).
[8] *Ibid.,* at para. 22.
[9] [1992] 3 S.C.R. 813 (S.C.C.) at 873.

The doctrine itself grew from a need to promote efficiency in the litigation process....One classic statement of the content and purpose of the doctrine is outlined in *Varcoe v. Lee*, 181 P. 223 (Cal. 1919) at p. 226:

> The three requirements...- that the matter be one of common and general knowledge, that it be well established and authoritatively settled, be practically indisputable, and that this common, general, and certain knowledge exist in the particular jurisdiction — all are requirements dictated by the reason and purpose of the rule, which is to obviate the formal necessity for proof when the matter does not require proof.

As Edumund M. Morgan noted in "Judicial Notice" (1944), 57 *Harv. L. Rev.* 269 at p. 272:

> ...the judge...must be assumed to have a fund of general information consisting of both generalized knowledge and knowledge of specific facts, and the capacity to relate it to what he has perceived during the proceeding, as well as the ability to draw reasonable deductions from the combination by using the ordinary processes of thought. That fund of general information must be at least as great as that of all reasonably well-informed persons in the community. He cannot be assumed to be ignorant of what is so generally accepted as to be incapable of dispute among reasonable men.

(b) What about "historical" facts?

Lamer J. for the court referred to the rule in *Sioui v. Quebec (Attorney General)*[10] in finding that judicial notice could be taken of 18th century documents such as military journals:[11]

> I am of the view that all the documents to which I will refer, whether my attention was drawn to them by the intervener or as a result of my personal research, are documents of a historical nature which I am entitled to rely on pursuant to the concept of judicial knowledge. As Norris J.A. said in *White and Bob* (at p. 629):
>
>> The Court is entitled "to take judicial notice of the facts of history whether past or contemporaneous" as Lord du Parcq said in *Monarch Steamship Co., Ltd. v. Karlshamns Oljefabriker (A/B)*, [1949] A.C. 196 at p. 234, [1949] 1 All E.R. 1 at p. 20, and it is entitled to rely on its own historical knowledge and researches, *Read v. Bishop of Lincoln*, [1892] A.C. 644, Lord Halsbury, L.C., at pp. 652-4.
>
> The documents I cite all enable the court, in my view, to identify more accurately the historical context essential to the resolution of this case.

---

[10] (sub nom. *R. v. Sioui)* [1990] 1 S.C.R. 1025 (S.C.C.).

[11] *Ibid.*, at 1050.

(c) Do *Charter* cases merit particular judicial notice?

In *R. v. Videoflicks Ltd.*,[13] an appeal concerning Sunday shopping laws, La Forest J. noted that despite the scanty evidence that had been presented concerning minority religious groups, counsel had freely discussed the religious practices of those groups during argument, and stated:[14]

> Besides, I do not accept that in dealing with broad social and economic facts such as those involved here the court is necessarily bound to rely solely on those presented by counsel. The admonition in *Oakes* and other cases to present evidence in *Charter* cases does not remove from the courts the power, where it deems it expedient, to take judicial notice of broad social and economic facts and to take the necessary steps to inform itself about them....There are, of course, dangers to judicial notice, but the alternatives in a case like this are to make an assumption without facts or to make a decision dependent on the evidence counsel has chosen to present. But as Marshall C.J. long ago reminded us, it is a *Constitution* we are interpreting. It is undesirable that an Act be found constitutional today and unconstitutional tomorrow simply on the basis of the particular evidence of broad social and economic facts that happens to have been presented by counsel. We should avoid this possibility when reasonably possible, particularly in these early days of *Charter* litigation when all are feeling their way regarding the manner in which *Charter* litigation is to be conducted.

3. Admissions

(a) In Civil Cases

Admissions in civil cases were considered by the British Columbia Court of Appeal in *Tunner v. Novak*,[15] a case in which it had been argued that the trial judge was wrong to rely on a fact in the defendant's affidavit, even though plaintiff's counsel had told the court that the facts alleged in the defendant's affidavit were accepted for the purposes of the summary trial application:[16]

> He says an admission or, to use his phrase, a provisional acceptance, of a fact cannot constitute a finding of fact. If he is right, the judgment is a nullity and there must be a new trial.

---

[13] (sub nom. *R. v. Edwards Books & Art Ltd.*) [1986] 2 S.C.R. 713 (S.C.C.).

[14] *Ibid.*, at 802-3, concurring.

[15] (1993), 76 B.C.L.R. (2d) 255 (B.C. C.A.).

[16] *Ibid.*, at 261-2, per Goldie J.A.

But this and similar objections fail in light of the purpose and effect of admissions. The relevant propositions are compendiously stated in "*The Law of Evidence in Canada*", 2nd ed. by Sopinka, Lederman and Bryant, (Butterworth's, Toronto, 1992) at p. 971:

> A formal admission in civil proceedings is a concession made by a party to the proceeding that a certain fact or issue is not in dispute. Formal admissions made for the purpose of dispensing with proof at trial are conclusive as to the matters admitted. As to these matters other evidence is precluded as being irrelevant, but, if such evidence is adduced the court is bound to act on the admission even if the evidence contradicts it. ...

> A formal admission may be made: (1) by a statement in the pleadings or by failure to deliver pleadings, (2) by an agreed statement of facts filed at the trial, (3) by an oral statement made by counsel at trial, or even counsel's silence in the face of statements made to the trial judge by the opposing counsel with the intention that the statements be relied on by the judge, (4) by a letter written by a party's solicitor prior to trial; or (5) by a reply or failure to reply to a request to admit facts.

In my view the concession made by counsel was a formal admission concurred in by the purchaser and the third parties. Accordingly, it was not open to the parties or the judge to controvert what was admitted for the purpose of dispensing with proof of the facts relied upon to establish the representation found by the chambers judge to be an innocent misrepresentation. In the circumstances of this case I think this extends to the third parties. Royal LePage and Ms. Bardell did not stand aloof at the summary trial. They contested the purchaser's allegations of misrepresentation vigorously, as they did in this Court. By so doing, they must be taken to have accepted the risk of an adverse finding. I think this is also so with respect to the purchaser's agents.

For the purposes of the summary trial and of this appeal findings of fact founded on the concession made by counsel are as though proof of the relevant facts had been tendered at trial.

(b) In Criminal Cases

Huddart J.A. considered admissions made in criminal trials in *R. v. Desjardins*:[17]

> In a criminal trial admissions may be made by an accused formally or informally. Formal admissions include:

---

[17] (1998), 110 B.C.A.C. 33 (B.C. C.A.) at 43.

(a) admissions of fact made in response to allegations of fact by the Crown under s. 655 of the *Criminal Code: R. v. Castellani*, [1970] S.C.R. 310; *R. v. Proctor* (1992), 69 C.C.C. (3d) 436 (Man. C.A.).

(b) an admission by way of a guilty plea that strict proof can be made that precludes the need for formal proof of an offence: *R. v. Adgey*, [1975] 2 S.C.R. 426; *R. v. Gardiner*, [1982] 2 S.C.R. 368.

Admissions of fact may also be contained in statements made by the accused in or out of court. When the statement is relevant to the issue of guilt, it may be described as a confession. These are informal admissions from which the court may find facts or draw inferences adverse to the accused without applying the rule for testimonial qualifications of personal knowledge: *R. v. Streu*, [1989] 1 S.C.R. 1521.

A peculiar type of admission is the co-conspirators' exception to the hearsay rule. This permits reception of evidence of what co-conspirators say out of court in furtherance of the conspiracy as an admission against all those participating in the conspiracy.[12]

4. Legislative Facts

It is difficult to know where in this volume a discussion of legislative facts might best be included. The topic does not fit neatly within a traditional framework. Its eventual inclusion in this section reflects the fact that while evidence of legislative facts may be adduced, it is not "proved" in the same strict sense as other evidence. The basic distinction in this regard between legislative facts and adjudicative facts was set out by Sopinka J. in *Danson v. Ontario (Attorney General)*:[18]

> It is necessary to draw a distinction at the outset between two categories of facts in constitutional litigation: "adjudicative facts" and "legislative facts". These terms derive from Davis, *Administrative Law Treatise* (1958), vol. 2, para. 15.03, p. 353. (See also Morgan, "Proof of Facts in Charter Litigation", in Sharpe, ed., *Charter Litigation* (1987).) Adjudicative facts are those that concern the immediate parties: in Davis's words, "who did what, where, when, how and with what motive or intent ...." Such facts are specific, and must be proved by admissible evidence. Legislative facts are those that establish the purpose and background of legislation, including its social, economic and cultural context. Such facts are of a more general nature, and are subject to less stringent admissibility requirements: see e.g., *Re Anti-Inflation Act*, [1976] 2 S.C.R. 373, per Laskin C.J., at p.

---

[12] See, for example, *R. v. Mapara*, [2005] 1 S.C.R. 358 (S.C.C.), which upheld the constitutionality of this rule.

[18] [1990] 2 S.C.R. 1086 (S.C.C.) at 1099.

391; *Re Residential Tenancies Act*, 1979, [1981] 1 S.C.R. 714, per Dickson J. (as he then was), at p. 723; and *Reference re Upper Churchill Water Rights Reversion Act*, [1984] 1 S.C.R. 297, per McIntyre J., at p. 318.

In *Canada Post Corp. v. Smith*,[19] a case in which the issue was the distinction between legislative and adjudicative facts and the proper means of adducing legislative facts in evidence, the Court quoted the above passage and added the following general discussion:[20]

> Trial-type procedures are best employed to resolve controversies involving disputes over adjudicative facts, facts pertaining to the parties. In contrast, such truth-seeking procedures are not usually required for the ascertainment of legislative facts. The exception is where specific or concrete legislative facts are critical to a judicial determination. Legislative facts relating more to policy than concrete fact are often not amenable to ascertainment by trial procedures. Cross-examining a social scientist on a particular theory is unlikely to produce a "truth" as understood in the context of adjudicative facts. Having regard to this reality which lies at the root of the variety of material that judges, since the inception of courts, have taken into account for the purposes of developing law or policy, the approach in the United States has been to confine the rules of evidence to adjudicative facts. Professor Kenneth Culp Davis, *Administrative Law Treatise*, 2nd ed., vol. 3 (1980), at p. 139, describes this policy in these terms:
>
> > The tradition for centuries has been that a court may not decide a disputed issue of fact about a party without evidence and without allowing opportunity for rebuttal and cross-examination. But when a court is confronted with a question of law or policy on which it needs facts to guide its judgment, the judicial custom over the centuries has been that the court may go anywhere for its facts. A court must bring wisdom to bear on issues of law and policy, but the needed wisdom is made up of multifarious ingredients that often defy identification and usually defy separation from other ingredients — knowledge of specific facts, understanding of general facts, prior experience in trying to solve similar problems, scientific information, mental processes such as logic or reasoning, mental processes such as appraising or estimating or guessing, formulation of notions about policy, imagination or inventiveness, intuition, controlled emotional reactions. Because of the intrinsic nature of the human mind, no possibility exists for creating law or policy without using mixtures of such ingredients, and no possibility exists of putting all of them into a party-prepared record of evidence. Judges who think creatively cannot confine their thoughts to facts that parties have prepared in a formal record of evidence.
>
> Professor Davis goes on to describe the implications of legislative fact for the law of evidence at p. 141 in these terms:

---

[19] (1994), 20 O.R. (3d) 173 (Ont. Div. Ct.).
[20] *Ibid.*, at 186-7.

The judicial practice of using extrarecord facts for deciding questions of law and policy is deeply established. It has been accepted by the legal profession without challenge. The leading legal scholars in the field of evidence have recognized the practice without questioning it. The deepest penetration may be that of Thayer, *A Preliminary Treatise on Evidence* 279 (1898): "In conducting a process of judicial reasoning, as of other reasoning, not a step can be taken without assuming something which has not been proved." As of nearly a century later, no one has even attempted to upset that profound observation; what inevitably follows is some such distinction as that between adjudicative and legislative facts, for judicial reasoning may be guided by facts that have not been proved but disputed facts about the parties must be proved. Wigmore was curiously somewhat baffled by the practice: "[I]n the course of appellate deliberations on the ordinary issues of law, modern realistic analysis has shown us that genuine questions of fact are sometimes dealt with . . . Assuming then, that . . . the Supreme Court has power to seek evidence for itself on facts which are beyond the scope of judicial notice, and to determine and find those facts for the purpose of reaching a conclusion of law, what rules of evidence shall it follow, if any, in that search? . . . All these are new questions, which have not yet been judicially answered, but are bound to be answered in the near future." 1 Wigmore, *Evidence* (3d ed. 1940) 145-46. Wigmore might better have said that one question is "judicially answered" by the universal practice of using extrarecord facts without any restriction by "rules of evidence." McCormick, *Evidence* 705 (1954), adopted the view of the present writer: "The usual resort . . . for ascertainment of **legislative facts** is not through a formal proof by sworn witnesses and authenticated documents but by the process of judicial notice." McCormick immediately made clear that the noticed facts need not be "certain and indisputable.

The exceptions to the need to adduce evidence that are dealt with above all reflect an easily-overlooked pragmatic side to evidence law and the judicial system. Presumptions, judicial notice and other alternatives to formal proof inherently recognize both the expense and onerous burden that would be imposed if strict proof were always required, and the common sense that members of the judiciary bring to the bench.

4

WHAT IS ITS WORTH?

Assuming that a proposed piece of evidence is, in fact, evidence, that counsel has managed to get it to court, and that it is necessary, the question arises of whether it is worth anything. This will involve considerations of relevance and weight, and possibly of materiality. Curiously, courts generally rely upon definitions of these terms found in texts or dictionaries, rather than going to definitions formulated by judges themselves. This may be because, as has been noted with regard to relevance, its determination is usually made by the application of experience and common sense rather than by a legal test.[1]

1. Relevance

The simplest and most fundamental concepts are the ones that can be most vexing to attempt to define. Perhaps this is why in an attempt to define "relevance", even the Supreme Court of Canada has taken the approach of quoting several different definitions in the hope that one of them may be apt:[2]

> Traditional definitions of what is relevant include "whatever accords with common sense" (McWilliams, Canadian Criminal Evidence (3rd ed. 1990), at p. 3-5); "'relevant' means that "any two facts to which it is applied are so related to each other that according to the common course of events one either taken by itself or in connection with other facts proves or renders probable the past, present or future existence or non-existence of the other" (Stephen's A Digest of the Law of Evidence (12th ed. 1946), art. 1), and finally Thayer's "logically probative" test with relevance as an affair of logic and not of law, a test adopted by this Court in Morris, infra.

> Whatever the test, be it one of experience, common sense or logic, it is a decision particularly vulnerable to the application of private beliefs. Regardless of the definition used, the content of any relevancy decision will be filled by the particular judge's experience, common sense and/or logic.

---

[1] Per Finch J.A., *R. v. Jabarianha* (1999), [1999] B.C.J. No. 2634, 1999 CarswellBC 2582 (B.C. C.A.), leave to appeal allowed (2000), 257 N.R. 396 (note) (S.C.C.) at para. 22, affirmed [2001] 3 S.C.R. 430 (S.C.C.).

[2] *R. v. Seaboyer*, [1991] 2 S.C.R. 577 (S.C.C.), at paras. 195-6.

In light of this approach, it makes sense to canvass the definitions that are most popular with the judiciary.

The following passage from Sopinka's *The Law of Evidence in Canada*, Toronto, 2nd ed., provides the definition of relevance that appears to be the one most frequently quoted by Canadian courts:[3]

> A traditionally accepted definition of relevance is that in Sir J.F. Stephen's *A Digest of the Law of Evidence* , where it is defined to mean:
>
>> ... any two facts to which it is applied are so related to each other that according to the common course of events one either taken by itself or in connection with other facts proves or renders probable the past, present, or future existence or non-existence of the other.
>
> Pratte J. in *R. v. Cloutier* accepted a definition from an early edition of *Cross on Evidence*:
>
>> For one fact to be relevant to another, there must be a connection or nexus between the two which makes it possible to infer the existence of one from the existence of the other. One fact is not relevant to another if it does not have real probative value with respect to the latter.

It must not be presumed that merely because evidence is relevant, that it necessarily follows that it is admissible. Relevant evidence can be excluded for many reasons, as discussed herein. As succinctly stated by Weiler J.A., "Relevance is a condition precedent to admissibility, but it does not determine admissibility."[4]

In addition to the above-quoted passage from Sopinka, with the quotes from Stephen and Pratte that it quotes in turn, another text that is frequently cited[5] for a definition of "relevance" is McWilliams, *Canadian Criminal Evidence*:

> Relevancy is also defined simply as whatever is logically probative or whatever accords with common sense.

---

[3] See for example, *R. v. Jabarianha, supra*, note 1; *Federal Business Development Bank v. Silver Spoon Desserts Enterprises Ltd.* (2000), [2000] N.S.J. No. 72, 2000 CarswellNS 64 (N.S. S.C. [In Chambers]), affirmed (2000), 4 C.P.C. (5th) 217 (N.S. C.A.) at para. 12; *Bank of Montreal v. 3D Properties Inc.* (1993), [1993] S.J. No. 279, 1993 CarswellSask 159 (Sask. Q.B.) at para. 10. Courts also frequently cite Sir J.F. Stephens' definition directly.

[4] *R. v. Peavoy* (1997), 117 C.C.C. (3d) 226 (Ont. C.A.).

[5] See, for example, *Coates v. Citizen (The)* (1986), 29 D.L.R. (4th) 523 (N.S. C.A.) at 532, per Pace J.A., dissenting in part.

As mentioned above, some judges prefer to quote dictionaries, such as Cusinato J. in *R. v. G. (L.J.)*:[6]

> In referring to the definition of relevance in *The Shorter Oxford English Dictionary*, Third Edition Revised, it is defined as "pertinent, applicable to the issue". Material evidence is defined as "evidence that proves or disproves an important view of the cause in dispute." In law, then, the material or the facts are important to perhaps influence or affect the result.

This tendency of the courts to rely on secondary sources is not because of any lack of judicial pronouncements on relevance. Lamer J., dissenting, but for a unanimous court on this point, clarified *Cloutier* in *R. v. Morris*:[7]

> It has been said that some might read in these comments (see Report of the Federal/Provincial Task Force on Uniform Rules of Evidence, at page 62 *et seq.*) a pronouncement by this court indicating a departure from *Thayer's* premise of relevancy, logic and experience and an adoption of *Wigmore's* concept of "legal relevancy" of which "the effect is to require a generally higher degree of probative value for all evidence to be submitted to a jury" and that "legal relevancy denotes, first of all, something more than a minimum of probative value. Each single piece of evidence must have a plus value" (1 Wigmore, *Evidence* #28.). I do not think that it was intended by the majority in this court in *Cloutier* that such a departure be made.

And further:[8]

> Thayer's (Thayer, *A preliminary treatise on evidence at the common law*, at p. 530.) statement of the law which is still the law in Canada, was as follows:

> (1) that nothing is to be received which is not logically probative of some matter requiring to be proved; and (2) that everything which is thus probative should come in, unless a clear ground of policy or law excludes it.

> To this general statement should be added the discretionary power judges exercise to exclude logically relevant evidence

> > as being of too slight a significance, or as having too conjectural and remote a connection; others, as being dangerous, in their effect on the jury and likely to be misused or overestimated by that body; others as being impolitic or unsafe on public grounds; others, on the bare ground of precedent. It is this

---

6 (1995), [1995] O.J. No. 1447, 1995 CarswellOnt 2780 (Ont. Gen. Div.), leave to appeal refused (1996), (sub nom. *Sexual Assault Crisis Centre of Essex County Inc. v. R.*) 90 O.A.C. 319 (note) (S.C.C.) at para. 16.

7 [1983] 2 S.C.R. 190 (S.C.C.) at 199.

8 *Ibid.*, at 201.

> sort of thing, as I said before, the rejection on one or another practical ground, of what is really probative, which is the characteristic thing in the law of evidence; stamping it as the child of the jury system. (Thayer, at p. 266)

It was through the exercise of this discretionary power that judges developed rules of exclusion. As said Thayer, at p. 265, when speaking of the rule of general admissibility of what is logically probative:

> ...in an historical sense it has not been the fundamental thing, to which the different exclusions were exceptions. What has taken place, in fact is the shutting out by the judges of one and another thing from time to time; and so, gradually, the recognition of this exclusion under a rule. These rules of exclusion have had their exceptions; and so the law has come into the shape of a set of primary rules of exclusion; and then a set of exceptions to these rules.

This passage from *Morris* was clarified by LaForest J., dissenting, in *R. v. Corbett*:[9]

> It should be noted that this passage followed a general discussion of the concept of relevance in which the Court affirmed that no minimum probative value is required for evidence to be deemed relevant. The Court made it clear that relevance does not involve considerations of sufficiency of probative value, and that, as McIntyre J., stated, at p. 192, "admissibility of evidence must not be confused with weight.". A cardinal principle of our law of evidence, then, is that any matter that has any tendency, as a matter of logic and human experience, to prove a fact in issue, is admissible in evidence, subject of course, to the overriding judicial discretion to exclude such matter for the practical and policy reasons already identified. Also important, especially in the context of the present case, is the Court's recognition that the present rules of exclusion are but specific accretions or manifestations of a subsisting general judicial discretion to exclude, on practical or policy grounds, that which is admittedly relevant.

Two attempts by Ontario judges to articulate their own definitions are also worth noting. In *R. v. Morin*,[10] Donnelly J. stated:[11]

> Relevant evidence is evidence which, either by itself or in conjunction with other evidence, tends to show the existence or non-existence of a fact in issue. There must be a logical nexus between the fact sought to be adduced and the matter about which the inference is to be drawn. The primary fact must be logically probative of the conclusionary fact. Evidence that is not probative of a fact in issue tends to prove nothing and is inadmissible. The general principle is that all relevant evidence is admissible subject to exclusionary considerations.

---

[9] [1988] 1 S.C.R. 670 (S.C.C.) at 715.

[10] (1991), [1991] O.J. No. 2528, 1991 CarswellOnt 5969 (Ont. Gen. Div.).

[11] *Ibid.*, [CarswellOnt] at para. 26.

Doherty J.A. in *R. v. Watson*[12] stated that "relevance":[13]

> ...requires a determination of whether as a matter of human experience and logic the existence of "Fact A" makes the existence or non-existence of "Fact B" more probable than it would be without the existence of Fact "A". If it does then "Fact A" is relevant to "Fact B". As long as "Fact B" is itself a material fact in issue or is relevant to a material fact in issue in the litigation, then "Fact A" is relevant and *prima facie* admissible.

Note that despite the references in several of the definitions provided above to the requirement that relevant evidence have a probative value, that probative value can apparently be very small:[14]

> To be logically relevant, an item of evidence does not have to firmly establish, on any standard, the truth or falsity of a fact in issue. The evidence must simply tend to "increase or diminish the probability of the existence of a fact in issue". See Sir Richard Eggleston, *Evidence, Proof and Probability* (2nd ed. 1978), at p. 83. As a consequence, there is no minimum probative value required for evidence to be relevant. See *R. v. Morris*, [1983] 2 S.C.R. 190, at pp. 199-200.

2. Relevance and Weight

Normally, relevance is the quality of proposed evidence that is considered in determining its admissibility, with weight to be determined later. This is noted — as is the exception for similar fact evidence — in the following passage by Cory J. in *R. v. Arp*:[15]

> As a general rule, a trial judge will admit evidence shown to be relevant, and will not engage in an evaluation of the probative value or weight of the evidence. If the trial judge is called on to make a preliminary finding of fact as a precondition to admissibility, this finding is usually unrelated to the quality or reliability of the evidence itself. See *R. v. Egger*, [1993] 2 S.C.R. 451, at p. 474. Indeed, the judge must refrain from evaluating the quality, weight or reliability of evidence when determining admissibility since the weight to be given to evidence is properly the province of the jury. See *R. v. Charemski*, [1998] 1 S.C.R. 679. However, in determining the admissibility of similar fact evidence the trial judge must, to a certain extent, invade this province. As Professor Smith stated in Case and Comment on *R. v. Hurren*, [1962] Crim. L.R. 770, at p. 771: It should be noted that judges commonly distinguish facts as going to weight rather than admissibility (see, e.g., *R. v. Wyatt*); but it is submitted that, as regards similar fact evidence, no sharp line can be drawn and that admissibility depends on weight.

---

[12] (1996), 30 O.R. (3d) 161 (Ont. C.A.).

[13] *Ibid.*, at 172.

[14] *R. v. Arp*, [1998] 3 S.C.R. 339 (S.C.C.) at 360, per Cory J. for the Court.

[15] *Ibid.* at 367.

3. Admissibility and Weight in Opinion Evidence

The distinction between admissibility and weight is of particular interest when some deficiency is alleged in expert opinion evidence. This distinction was considered in *R. v. Abbey*,[16] *R. v. Lavallee*,[17] and *R. v. Warsing*.[18] Major J. summed up the distinction in *Warsing*:[19]

> In many cases the evidence of experts depends on the hypothesis or assumptions that they are asked to make. The value of the opinion will depend on the validity of the assumptions and is related to weight not admissibility.

> The appellant's submissions on the strict application of the rule in *Abbey* should be assessed in light of Wilson J.'s later decision in *Lavallee*, which considered *Abbey*. Wilson J., there, set out four propositions which represented the ratio of *Abbey* (at p. 893):

> 1. An expert opinion is admissible if relevant, even if it is based on second-hand evidence.

> 2. This second hand evidence (hearsay) is admissible to show the information on which the expert opinion is based, not as evidence going to the existence of the facts on which the opinion is based.

> 3. Where the psychiatric evidence is comprised of hearsay evidence, the problem is the weight to be attributed to the opinion.

> 4. Before any weight can be given to an expert's opinion, the facts upon which the opinion is based must be found to exist.

> Wilson J. in considering the fourth principle held that as long as there is some admissible evidence on which the expert's testimony is based it cannot be ignored; but it follows that the more the expert relies on facts not in evidence, the weight given to the opinion will diminish.

4. Materiality

Materiality is a much less frequently encountered term than relevance in evidentiary arguments. This may be because the question of whether or not evidence is directed at a matter in issue is more apparent and less a matter for argument than the question of whether or not it is

---

[16] [1982] 2 S.C.R. 24 (S.C.C.).
[17] [1990] 1 S.C.R. 852 (S.C.C.).
[18] [1998] 3 S.C.R. 579 (S.C.C.).
[19] *Ibid.* at 608-9.

probative of some matter at issue. For this reason, materiality is a concept which is more likely to arise in cases dealing with issues in the specialized fields of insurance or accounting than evidence generally.

When a definition of materiality is needed, the courts may turn to dictionaries, as in *Wingold v. W. B. Sullivan Construction Ltd.*, per Hughes J.:[20]

> In the *Shorter Oxford English Dictionary* two meanings deriving from the 16th century are eminently applicable; "of much consequence; important." and "pertinent, germane, or essential to". Then as appertaining particularly to "Law, etc.";
> "Of such significance as to be likely to influence the determination of a cause, to alter the character of an instrument, etc." The proper meaning and its application to the words of the section generally was a matter for discussion in argument.

In considering the production of clinical records in sexual assault trials in *A. (L.L.) v. B. (A.)*,[21] L'Heureux-Dubé J. noted the following with regard to materiality in summarizing the submissions of one of the parties:[22]

> The procedure would be initiated by subpoena *duces tecum* and the threshold test would be the likely materiality of the records, *i.e.*, that they are capable of affecting the outcome of the trial. Likely materiality must be determined with regard to the purpose to which the evidence is put and must be based on a proper factual foundation. Hypothetical allegations based on erroneous assumptions informed by stereotypes and myths would be inappropriate and unfair to sexual assault complainants.

A slightly broader test of materiality in a criminal context was stated in *R. v. Jarema*,[23] which was quoted with approval by the Supreme Court of Canada in *R. v. Taillefer*:[24]

> In *Jarema, supra*, the Alberta Court of Appeal had to examine precisely that question: the validity of a guilty plea in the context of the Crown's breach of its duty to disclose. The court stated the test applicable in such a situation involving the actual decision to plead guilty, when assessed within the entire context of the case, as follows (at para. 24):
>
> > The Crown in this case did fail to disclose some information which it ought to have disclosed. The Crown concedes this fact. The question is whether the accused has met the most favourable possible test for him. That is a

---

[20] (May 25, 1981), Doc. 6532/76, 12374/77, [1981] O.J. No. 239 (Ont. H.C.).

[21] [1995] 4 S.C.R. 536 (S.C.C.).

[22] *Ibid.*, at 549.

[23] (1996), 43 Alta. L.R. (3d) 345 (Alta. C.A.).

[24] [2003] 3 S.C.R. 307 (S.C.C.) at para. 89.

> *reasonable possibility* that this non-disclosure impaired his right to full answer and defense. From the perspective of an appellate court, this in turn requires an assessment of materiality, by asking whether there is a reasonable possibility that the outcome of the trial would have been different if the information had been disclosed. In the context of a guilty plea by the accused, this materiality question must be modified slightly: the Court must evaluate whether there is a reasonable possibility either that the accused's choice to plead guilty would have been [p. 349] different, or that the undisclosed information undermines the validity of the guilty pleas: see *R. v. T. (R.)* (1992), 17 C.R. (4th) 247 at 262 (Ont. C.A.).

In concluding this consideration of relevance, weight and materiality, it must be noted that even experienced counsel can easily confuse these fundamental concepts. When this happens, arguments can, for example, arise over the relevance of evidence that is only introduced for its materiality, or counsel may find themselves arguing for the exclusion of evidence that should instead be admitted but accorded little weight. In some ways, the specific evidentiary issues that are considered in subsequent chapters can be easier to grasp than these more fundamental principles of evidence law.

5. Evidential Burden

An issue that arises with regard to the worth of evidence in jury trials is that of whether the "evidential burden" has been discharged. That is, has evidence been led upon which a properly instructed jury could reasonably decide the issue? If it has, then the judge refers the issue to the jury without evaluating the quality, weight or reliability of the evidence. The jury then determines whether the "persuasive burden" has been discharged in arriving at their decision as to how the issue should be decided. While the Supreme Court of Canada has said that this principle has been "unaltered in substance for at least a century", it acknowledges that it has been "variously attired".[25] This is true both of the general principle — *i.e.* ". . .that the evidential burden is discharged *if there is some evidence upon which a properly instructed jury could reasonably decide the issue. . .*"[26] — and of the concepts of evidential burden and persuasive burden, which have spawned the synonyms listed by Dickson C.J. and quoted by McLachlin C.J. and Bastarache J. in their discussion of the formulation as the "air of reality test":[27]

---

[25] *R. v. Fontaine*, [2004] 1 S.C.R. 702 (S.C.C.) at para. 13.

[26] *Ibid.*, at para. 14 [underlining in original].

[27] *R. v. Cinous*, [2002] 2 S.C.R. 3 (S.C.C.) at para. 52.

It is trite law that the air of reality test imposes a burden on the accused that is merely evidential, rather than persuasive. Dickson C.J. drew attention to the distinction between these two types of burden in *R. v. Schwartz*, [1988] 2 S.C.R. 443, at p. 466:

> Judges and academics have used a variety of terms to try to capture the distinction between the two types of burdens. The burden of establishing a case has been referred to as the "major burden," the "primary burden," the "legal burden" and the "persuasive burden."*The burden of putting an issue in play has been called the "minor burden," the "secondary burden," the "evidential burden," the "burden of going forward," and the "burden of adducing evidence."* [Emphasis added.]

The air of reality test is concerned only with whether or not a putative defence should be "put in play", that is, submitted to the jury for consideration.

5
SHOULD IT BE EXCLUDED?

1. Hearsay

It may seem to some observers that the law of evidence is intended to prevent evidence from being adduced that "common sense" would demand be admitted. Indeed, it may seem that the law of evidence is entirely about excluding evidence. It is clear, however, that the law of evidence as a whole, including its exclusionary aspects, operate to safeguard the fairness of our legal system rather than to frustrate it. As observed by L'Heureux-Dubé J. (dissenting in part) in *R. v. Seaboyer*:[1]

> . . .parameters developed at common law, which restrict admissibility, go further towards safeguarding fairness than does their absence. As La Forest J. proposed in *Corbett*, supra, at p. 744 [[1988] 1 S.C.R.], "the principle of relevancy. . . helps to ensure that the trial is conducted fairly and that justice is done." Relevance along with other exclusionary rules developed at common law have had an important hand in shaping the notion of "fairness".

(a) What is Hearsay?

A concise definition was stated by Sopinka J. in *R. v. Dipietro*:[2]

> An out-of-court statement which is admitted for the truth of its contents is hearsay. An out-of-court statement offered simply as proof that the statement was made is not hearsay, and is admissible as long as it has some probative value.

A longer definition which is frequently quoted with approval (*e.g.* in *R. v. Smith*)[3] is found in *Subramaniam v. Public Prosecutor*:[4]

> Evidence of a statement made to a witness by a person who is not himself called as a witness may or may not be hearsay. It is hearsay and inadmissible when the

---

[1] [1991] 2 S.C.R. 577 (S.C.C.) at para. 249.
[2] (sub nom. *R. v. Evans*) [1993] 3 S.C.R. 653 (S.C.C.) at 661-2.
[3] [1992] 2 S.C.R. 915 (S.C.C.) at 924.
[4] [1956] 1 W.L.R. 965 (Malaysia P.C.) at 970.

object of the evidence is to establish the truth of what is contained in the statement. It is not hearsay and is admissible when it is proposed to establish by the evidence, not the truth of the statement, but the fact that it was made. The fact that the statement was made, quite apart from its truth, is frequently relevant in considering the mental state and conduct thereafter of the witness or of some other person in whose presence the statement was made.

(b) The Traditional Applications of the Hearsay Rule

As noted by McLachlin J. in *R. v. Khan*:[5]

The hearsay rule has traditionally been regarded as an absolute rule, subject to various categories of exceptions, such as admissions, dying declarations, declarations against interest and spontaneous declarations. While this approach has provided a degree of certainty to the law on hearsay, it has frequently proved unduly inflexible in dealing with new situations and new needs in the law.

(c) Creation of the Contemporary Rule

In *R. v. Khan*,[6] a 4-year-old girl had told her mother details of a sexual assault by the accused physician. At trial, the accused was acquitted after the judge held that the girl was incompetent to testify and that her mother's statements about what the girl had told her were inadmissible as hearsay. The Supreme Court of Canada held that the mother's evidence of what the girl had told her was admissible, adopting a more flexible approach to hearsay based upon necessity and reliability:[7]

The first question should be whether reception of the hearsay statement is necessary. Necessity for these purposes must be interpreted as "reasonably necessary". The inadmissibility of the child's evidence might be one basis for a finding of necessity. But sound evidence based on psychological assessments that testimony in court might be traumatic for the child or harm the child might also serve. There may be other examples of circumstances which could establish the requirement of necessity.

The next question should be whether the evidence is reliable. Many considerations such as timing, demeanour, the personality of the child, the intelligence and understanding of the child, and the absence of any reason to expect fabrication in the statement may be relevant on the issue of reliability. I would not wish to draw up a strict list of considerations for reliability, nor to suggest that certain categories of evidence (for example the evidence of young children on sexual encounters)

---

[5] [1990] 2 S.C.R. 531 (S.C.C.) at 540.

[6] *Ibid.*

[7] *Ibid.*, at 546-8.

should be always regarded as reliable. The matters relevant to reliability will vary with the child and with the circumstances, and are best left to the trial judge.

In determining the admissibility of the evidence, the judge must have regard to the need to safeguard the interests of the accused....in most cases the concerns of the accused as to credibility will remain to be addressed by submissions as to the weight to be accorded to the evidence, and submissions as to the quality of any corroborating evidence....

I conclude that hearsay evidence of a child's statement on crimes committed against the child should be received, provided that the guarantees of necessity and reliability are met, subject to such safeguards as the judge may consider necessary and subject always to considerations affecting the weight that should be accorded to such evidence.

While it could have initially appeared that the approach in *Khan* might be restricted to cases involving testimony by children, it was later made absolutely clear that this approach was to be one of general application in *R. v. Smith*,[8] per Lamer C.J.C.:[9]

This court has not taken the position that the hearsay rule precludes the reception of hearsay evidence unless it falls within established categories of exceptions, such as "present intentions" or state of mind". Indeed in our recent decision in *R. v. Khan*, we indicated that the categorical approach to exceptions to the hearsay rule has the potential to undermine, rather than further, the policy of avoiding the frailties of certain types of evidence which the hearsay rule was originally fashioned to avoid....
The decision of this court in *Khan*, therefore, should be understood as the triumph of a principled analysis over a set of ossified judicially created categories....

Clearly, the facts of *Khan* are not similar to the facts on the present appeal....In the present case, the declarant would have been a competent witness had she been available to give evidence, but she is dead. However *Khan* should not be understood as turning on its particular facts, but, instead, must be seen as a particular expression of the fundamental principles that underlie the hearsay rule and the exceptions to it. What is important, in my view, is the departure signalled by *Khan* from a view of hearsay characterized by a general prohibition on the reception of such evidence, subject to a limited number of defined categorical exceptions, and a movement towards an approach governed by the principles which underlie the rule and its exceptions alike. The movement towards a flexible approach was motivated by the realization that, as a general rule, reliable evidence ought not to be excluded simply because it cannot be tested by cross-examination. The preliminary determination of reliability is to be made exclusively by the trial judge before the evidence is admitted.

---

[8] [1992] 2 S.C.R. 915 (S.C.C.).
[9] *Ibid.*, at 928-33.

The court's decision in *Khan*, therefore, signalled an end to the old categorical approach to the admission of hearsay evidence. Hearsay evidence is now admissible on a principled basis, the governing principles being the reliability of the evidence and its necessity.

(d) A Concise Statement of the Contemporary Rule

At the time of writing, the most recent overview by the Supreme Court of Canada was provided in *R. v. Mapara*:[10]

> The principled approach to the admission of hearsay evidence which has emerged in this Court over the past two decades attempts to introduce a measure of flexibility into the hearsay rule to avoid these negative outcomes. Based on the *Starr* decision, the following framework emerges for considering the admissibility of hearsay evidence:
>
> (a) Hearsay evidence is presumptively inadmissible unless it falls under an exception to the hearsay rule. The traditional exceptions to the hearsay rule remain presumptively in place.
>
> (b) A hearsay exception can be challenged to determine whether it is supported by indicia of necessity and reliability, required by the [page 367] principled approach. The exception can be modified as necessary to bring it into compliance.
>
> (c) In "rare cases", evidence falling within an existing exception may be excluded because the indicia of necessity and reliability are lacking in the particular circumstances of the case.
>
> (d) If hearsay evidence does not fall under a hearsay exception, it may still be admitted if indicia of reliability and necessity are established on a *voir dire*.

(e) The Two Criteria: Reliability and Necessity

In *Smith*,[11] Lamer C.J.C. also elaborated on the two criteria identified in *Khan*[12] as requiring admission of hearsay evidence:[13]

> The criterion of "reliability" — or, in Wigmore's terminology, the circumstantial guarantee of trustworthiness — is a function of the circumstances under which the statement in question was made. If a statement sought to be adduced by way

---

[10] [2005] 1 S.C.R. 358 (S.C.C.) at para. 15.
[11] *Supra*, note 8.
[12] *Supra*, note 5.
[13] *Supra*, note 8, at 933-4.

of hearsay evidence is made under circumstances which substantially negate the possibility that the declarant was untruthful or mistaken, the hearsay evidence may be said to be "reliable", *i.e.*, a circumstantial guarantee of trustworthiness is established. The evidence of the infant complainant in *Khan* was found to be reliable on this basis.

The companion criterion of "necessity" refers to the necessity of the hearsay evidence to prove a fact in issue. Thus, in *Khan*, the infant complainant was found by the trial judge not to be competent to testify herself. In this sense, hearsay evidence of her statements was necessary, in that what she said to her mother could not be adduced through her. It was her inability to testify that governed the situation.

The criterion of necessity, however, does not have the sense of "necessary to the prosecution's case". If this were the case, uncorroborated hearsay evidence which satisfied the criterion of reliability would be admissible if uncorroborated, but might no longer be "necessary" to the prosecution's case if corroborated by other independent evidence. Such an interpretation of the criterion of "necessity" would thus produce the illogical result that uncorroborated hearsay evidence would be admissible, but could become inadmissible if corroborated. This is not what was intended by this court's decision in *Khan*.

As indicated above, the criterion of necessity must be given a flexible definition, capable of encompassing diverse situations. What these situations will have in common is that the relevant direct evidence is not, for a variety of reasons, available. Necessity of this nature may arise in a number of situations. Wigmore, while not attempting an exhaustive enumeration, suggested at §1421 the following categories:

(1) The person whose assertion is offered may now be dead, or out of the jurisdiction, or insane, or otherwise unavailable for the purpose of testing [by cross-examination]. This is the commoner and more palpable reason....

(2) The assertion may be such that we cannot expect, again or at this time, to get evidence of the same value from the same or other sources....The necessity is not so great; perhaps hardly a necessity, only an expediency or convenience, can be predicated. But the principle is the same.

Clearly the categories of necessity are not closed.

(f) Admissions of a Party

The traditional exception to the hearsay rule for out-of-court admissions by a party[14] was affirmed in *R. v. Terry*,[15] per McLachlin J. where evidence of a poem and a dream about stabbing had been admitted in the murder trial of the accused:[16]

> An admission against interest made by the accused is admissible as a recognized exception to the hearsay rule, provided that its probative value outweighs its prejudicial effect.

(g) Business Records

A number of criteria had to be met in order to satisfy the business records exception under the common law. Laycraft C.J.A. noted these in *R. v. Monkhouse*:[17]

> Wigmore defined no less than seven criteria to be satisfied at common law for the admission, as evidence of the truth of its contents, of a document containing hearsay. These were that the hearsay portion must be (1) an original entry, (2) made contemporaneously with that which it recorded, (3) in the routine, (4) of business, (5) by a person since deceased, (6) who was under a duty to do the act and record it and (7) who had no motive to misrepresent it. (Wigmore, 3rd Ed., Vol. 5, Sections 1517 and 1521-35.)

The Court in that case noted, however, that the contemporary Canadian version of the common law business records exception was somewhat different:[18]

> In his useful book, Documentary Evidence in Canada (Carswell Co., 1984), Mr. J.D. Ewart summarizes the common law rule after the decision in *Ares v. Venner*[19] as follows at page 54:
>
>> the modern rule can be said to make admissible a record containing (i) an original entry (ii) made contemporaneously (iii) in the routine (iv) of business (v) by a recorder with personal knowledge of the thing recorded as a result of having done or observed or formulated it (vi) who had a duty to make the

---

[14] Note that the common usage is that "admissions against interest" are made by a party, while "declarations against interest" are made by a non-party.

[15] [1996] 2 S.C.R. 207 (S.C.C.).

[16] *Ibid.*, at 220.

[17] (1987), [1988] 1 W.W.R. 725 (Alta. C.A.) at 730.

[18] *Ibid.*, at 732.

[19] [1970] S.C.R. 608 (S.C.C.).

record and (vii) who had no motive to misrepresent. Read in this way, the rule after *Ares* does reflect a more modern, realistic approach for the common law to take towards business duty records.

> To this summary, I would respectfully make one modification. The "original entry" need not have been made personally by a recorder with knowledge of the thing recorded. On the authority of *Omand*,[20] *Ashdown*,[21] and *Moxley*,[22] it is sufficient if the recorder is functioning in the usual and ordinary course of a system in effect for the preparation of business records.

Of course, the importance of the common law business records exception is greatly diminished by provisions in the various *Evidence Act*s allowing for the admission of business records. In addition, the business records exception has now been explicitly held to be subject to the principled analysis of hearsay evidence as set out in *R. v. Khan*.[23] Application of the principled approach led L'Heureux-Dubé J. in dissent to speculate that perhaps the business records exemption should be re-examined in cases where the records have been written by persons who are not disinterested parties.[24]

(h) Declarations Against Interest

In *R. v. Demeter*,[25] Martland J. for the majority quoted from the Ontario Court of Appeal in stating the traditional exception to the hearsay rule for declarations against interest:[26]

> At common law an oral or written declaration against pecuniary or proprietary interest by a deceased declarant has been long held to be admissible to prove the fact declared.

The exception for declarations against pecuniary interest had not, however, previously extended to declarations against penal interest, although the same rationale might be seen to apply. The exception was therefore extended in *R. v. O'Brien*:[27]

---

[20] *Omand v. Alberta Milling Co.*, [1922] 3 W.W.R. 412 (Alta. C.A.).
[21] *J.H. Ashdown Hardware Co. v. Singer* (1951), [1952] 1 D.L.R. 33 (Alta. C.A.), affirmed [1953] 1 S.C.R. 252 (S.C.C.).
[22] *Moxley v. Canada Atlantic Railway* (1888), 15 S.C.R. 145 (S.C.C.).
[23] *R. v. Owen*, [2003] 1 S.C.R. 779 (S.C.C.) at para. 59.
[24] *R. v. Starr*, [2000] 2 S.C.R. 144 (S.C.C.) at para. 57.
[25] (1977), [1978] 1 S.C.R. 538 (S.C.C.).
[26] *Ibid.*, at 542.
[27] (1977), [1978] 1 S.C.R. 591 (S.C.C.) at 599, per Dickson J. for the Court.

There is little or no reason why declarations against penal interest and those against pecuniary or proprietary interest should not stand on the same footing. A person is as likely to speak the truth in a matter affecting his liberty as in a matter affecting his pocketbook. For these reasons and the ever-present possibility that a rule of absolute prohibition could lead to grave injustice I would hold that, in a proper case, a declaration against penal interest is admissible according to the law of Canada;...

The conditions for a declaration against penal interest to be received in evidence were set out in *R. v. Lucier*:[28]

1. The declaration would have to be made to such a person and in such circumstances that the declarant should have apprehended a vulnerability to penal consequences as a result. In *Sussex Peerage* the Lord Chancellor would not have admitted the declaration in any event of the rule because it was made to the declarant's son. In ordinary circumstances where a declaration is made for instance to an unestranged son, wife or mother, the psychological assurance of reliability is lacking because of [sic] risk of penal consequences is not real and the declarant may have motives such as a desire for self-aggrandizement or to shock which makes the declaration unreliable.

2. The vulnerability to penal consequences would have to be not remote.

3. "...the declaration sought to be given in evidence must be considered in its totality. If upon the whole tenor the weight is in favour of the declarant, it is not against his interest": *Re Van Beelen*, p. 208; *R. v. Agawa* (1975), 11 O.R. (2d) 176.

4. In a doubtful case a Court might properly consider whether or not there are other circumstances connecting the declarant with the crime and whether or not there is any connection between the declarant and the accused.

5. The declarant would have to be unavailable by reason of death, insanity, grave illness which prevents the giving of testimony even from a bed, or absence in a jurisdiction to which none of the processes of the Court extends.

(i) Dying Declarations

The Supreme Court of Canada considered dying declarations in *R. v. Schwartzenhauer*.[29] It noted several requirements for the operation of this common law exception to the hearsay rule. Per Davis J.:[30]

As early as 1824, in *The King v. Mead* [(1824) 2 Barn. & Cres. 605.] Abbott C.J. stated the general rule that evidence of dying declarations is only admissible where the death of the deceased is the subject of the charge and the circumstances of the death the subject of the dying declaration.

---

28 [1982] 1 S.C.R. 28 (S.C.C.) at 32.
29 [1935] S.C.R. 367 (S.C.C.).
30 *Ibid.*, at 369.

And:[31]

> Clearly, dying declarations are competent only in homicidal cases, and then only in so far as the statements therein could have been given in evidence by the deceased had she lived.

And per Cannon J.:[32]

> ...whether the deceased had such a belief of impending death as to make her declaration admissible as a dying declaration...

Note, however, that, L'Heureux-Dubé J. dissenting, in *obiter* speculated that courts "may wish to reconsider the dying declaration under certain circumstances such as when a dying person is under the influence of powerful drugs."[33]

(j) Prior Identification

The prior identification exception to the hearsay rule was referred to by Iacobucci J. for the majority in *R. v. Starr*:[34]

> The scope of the "prior identification" exception to the hearsay rule was recently thoroughly canvassed in the lucid reasons of Doherty J.A. in *Tat*,[35] *supra*. As Doherty J.A. sets out, there are two situations in which out-of-court statements of identification may be admitted for the truth of their contents. First, "prior statements identifying or describing the accused are admissible where the identifying witness identifies the accused at trial" (pp. 497-98). Second, such statements are admissible "where the identifying witness is unable to identify the accused at trial, but can testify that he or she previously gave an accurate description or made an accurate identification" (p. 500). In the latter circumstance, Doherty J.A. explained, "the identifying witness may testify to what he or she said or did on those earlier occasions and those who heard the description given by the witness or witnessed the identification made by the witness may give evidence of what the witness said or did" (*ibid.*).

(k) Prior Testimony

Although there had been some debate about whether testimony in a prior proceeding constituted hearsay, Lamer C.J. found that it did, but

---

[31] *Ibid.*, at 370.

[32] *Ibid.*, at 372.

[33] *Supra*, note 24, at para. 57.

[34] [2000] 2 S.C.R. 144 (S.C.C.) at 256.

[35] *R. v. Tat* (1997), 117 C.C.C. (3d) 481 (Ont. C.A.).

that there was a recognized common law exception for prior testimony in *R. v. Hawkins*:[36]

> The testimony of a declarant in a prior proceeding, *prima facie*, raises a hearsay danger because the trier of fact cannot examine the demeanour of the declarant at trial. Indeed, if such testimony did not represent hearsay, there would be no need for provisions similar to s. 715, as such prior testimony would be substantively admissible in all circumstances, even if the declarant was otherwise available to testify.
>
> Regardless of the appropriate characterization of such former testimony, the common law was historically prepared to admit such evidence either as non-hearsay or as an exception to the hearsay rule in specific circumstances where the declarant was generally unavailable to testify at trial.

(l) Public Documents

The common law exception to the hearsay rule for public documents was noted by Rand J. in *R. v. Finestone*:[37]

> The argument made to us somewhat confused the admissibility of an entry made strictly in the course of business and one made pursuant to a public duty. The rule in relation to the latter does not seem ever to have been doubted. As early as 1785 in *R. v. Aickles* [(1785) 1 Leach Cr. L. 390 at 392.], it is said:
>
>> The law reposes such a confidence in public officers that it presumes they will discharge their several trusts with accuracy and fidelity; and therefore whatever acts they do in discharge of their public duty may be given in evidence and shall be taken to be true, under such a degree of caution as the nature and circumstances of each case may appear to require.
>
> In *Doe v. France* [15 Q.B. 758.], Erle J. says:
>
>> It depends upon the public duty of the person who keeps the register to make such entries in it, after satisfying himself of their truth.

A comprehensive review of the rationale for the rule was delivered by Klebuc J. in the course of holding that a publication by Statistics Canada could be received in evidence without any expert testimony confirming its validity.[38]

---

[36] [1996] 3 S.C.R. 1043 (S.C.C.) at 1078-9.
[37] [1953] 2 S.C.R. 107 (S.C.C.) at 109.
[38] *Daum v. Schroeder* (1996), [1996] S.J. No. 406, 1996 CarswellSask 440 (Sask. Q.B.).

(m) *Res Gestae*

The *res gestae* exception to the hearsay rule was recognized by the Supreme Court of Canada as early as 1907.[39] An explanation of the rationale for the exception that has sometimes been adopted by Canadian courts is from *Wigmore*:[40]

> This general principle is based on the experience that, under certain external circumstances of physical shock, a stress of nervous excitement may be produced which stills the reflective faculties and removes their control, so that the utterance which then occurs is a spontaneous and sincere response to the actual sensations and perceptions already produced by the external shock. Since this utterance is made under the immediate and uncontrolled domination of the senses, and during the brief period when considerations of self-interest could not have been brought fully to bear by reasoned reflection, the utterance may be taken as particularly trustworthy (or at least as lacking the usual grounds of untrustworthiness), and thus as expressing the real tenor of the speaker's belief as to the facts just observed by him; and may therefore be received as testimony to those facts.

Wigmore's explanation is most obviously relevant to the instances of criminal assault which have often given rise to the application of the rule in such well known cases as *Gilbert v. R.*,[41] *R. v. Leland*,[42] *R. v. Clark*[43] and *Ratten v. R.*[44] The latter case, which has been found to be generally accepted as part of Canadian law,[45] shifted the emphasis for determining whether the *res gestae* exception applies from the contemporaneity of the statement to the likelihood that the spontaneity of the statement means that it was not concocted:[46]

> The possibility of concoction, or fabrication, where it exists, is on the other hand an entirely valid reason for exclusion, and is probably the real test which judges in fact apply. In their Lordships' opinion this should be recognised and applied directly as the relevant test: the test should be not the uncertain one whether the making of the statement was in some sense part of the event or transaction. This may often be difficult to establish: such external matters as the time which elapses

---

[39] *R. v. Gilbert* (1907), 38 S.C.R. 284 (S.C.C.).

[40] See, for example, *R. v. Suzack* (2000), [2000] O.J. No. 100, 2000 CarswellOnt 95 (Ont. C.A.) at [O.J.] para. 26, leave to appeal refused (2001), 80 C.R.R. (2d) 376 (note) (S.C.C.); *R. v. F. (G.)* (1999), 43 O.R. (3d) 290 (Ont. C.A.) at 299.

[41] (1907), 38 S.C.R. 207 (S.C.C.).

[42] (1950), [1951] O.R. 12 (Ont. C.A.).

[43] (1983), 42 O.R. (2d) 609 (Ont. C.A.), leave to appeal refused (1983), 42 O.R. (2d) 609 (note) (S.C.C.).

[44] [1971] 3 All E.R. 801 (Australia P.C.).

[45] *R. v. Crossley* (1997), [1997] B.C.J. No. 1783, 1997 CarswellBC 1677 (B.C. C.A.) at para. 15.

[46] *Rattan, supra*, note 44, at 807.

between the events and the speaking of the words (or vice versa), and differences in location being relevant factors but not, taken by themselves, decisive criteria. As regards statements made after the event it must be for the judge, by preliminary ruling, to satisfy himself that the statement was so clearly made in circumstances of spontaneity or involvement in the event that the possibility of concoction can be disregarded. Conversely, if he considers that the statement was made by way of narrative of a detached prior event so that the speaker was so disengaged from it as to be able to construct or adapt his account, he should exclude it. And the same must in principle be true of statements made before the event. The test should be not the uncertain one, whether the making of the statement should be regarded as part of the event or transaction. This may often be difficult to show. But if the drama, leading up to the climax, has commenced and assumed such intensity and pressure that the utterance can safely be regarded as a true reflection of what was unrolling or actually happening, it ought to be received. The expression '*res gestae*' may conveniently sum up these criteria, but the reality of them must always be kept in mind: it is this that lies behind the best reasoned of the judges' rulings.

Note that some writers on evidence law subsume the state of mind exception to the hearsay rule under *res gestae*; see the following section for a discussion of that exception. It is also sometimes suggested that there is a *res gestae* exception for declarations of bodily feeling and conditions.[47]

For proof that the *res gestae* exception continues to be good law, see *R. v. Mapara*, in which the majority of the Court reasoned that the co-conspirators' exception to the hearsay rule was justifiable by analogy to the *res gestae* exception to the hearsay rule, in that surrounding context furnishes circumstantial indicators of reliability.[48]

(n) State of Mind

The "state of mind" or "present intentions" exception to the hearsay rule was summarized by Iacobucci J. in *R. v. Starr*:[49]

> In *Smith*, Lamer C.J. explained that the exception as it has developed in Canada permits the admission into evidence of statements of intent or of other mental states for the truth of their contents and also, in the case of statements of intention in particular, to support an inference that the declarant followed through on the intended course of action, provided it is reasonable on the evidence for the trier

---

[47] See Sopinka, Lederman and Bryant, *The Law of Evidence in Canada*, 2nd ed. (Toronto: Butterworths, 1999), p. 252 citing cases such as *Youlden v. London Guarantee & Accident Co.* (1912), 26 O.L.R. 75 (Ont. H.C.), affirmed (1913), 12 D.L.R. 433 (Ont. C.A.).

[48] *Supra*, note 10, at paras. 24-6.

[49] [2000] 2 S.C.R. 144 (S.C.C.) at 232-3.

of fact to infer that the declarant did so. At the same time, there are certain inferences that may not permissibly be drawn from hearsay evidence of the out-of-court declarant's intentions. On this point, Lamer C.J. cited with approval (at p. 927) from the judgment of Doherty J. in *P. (R.)*,[50] *supra*, at pp. 343-44, where the case law was summarized as follows:

> The evidence is not, however, admissible to show the state of mind of persons other than the deceased (unless they were aware of the statements), or to show that persons [page 233] other than the deceased acted in accordance with the deceased's stated intentions, save perhaps cases where the act was a joint one involving the deceased and another person. The evidence is also not admissible to establish that past acts or events referred to in the utterances occurred.

> As noted by J. Sopinka, S. N. Lederman and A. W. Bryant, in *The Law of Evidence in Canada* (2nd ed. 1999), at para. 6.236, in *Smith* the Court adopted "the proposition that the admissibility of statements of intention were to be limited to the declarant's state of mind and could not be used to prove the act or intention of any other person". It is important to emphasize that even in "cases where the act was a joint one involving the deceased and another person", the hearsay is not generally admissible to show the intentions of a third party.

In concluding a discussion on hearsay, it must be said that this is the subject that seems most likely to lead to confusion in evidentiary arguments, so that counsel find themselves, for example, arguing that some proposed evidence is not hearsay when it clearly is hearsay, and they should actually be arguing about its admissibility under an exception to the hearsay rule. It is important to remember that establishing that a piece of evidence is hearsay is not the end of the matter, and to consider whether an exception on the grounds of reliability and necessity or one of the traditional exceptions to the hearsay rule applies.

2. Oral History, A Special Case

An emerging issue in the law of evidence is the proper treatment of oral history in Aboriginal cases. A discussion of this topic could have been included in the preceding section on hearsay. After all, evidence that may, for example, be along the lines of "my grandmother told me that our ancestors have always fished at this spot" or "when this treaty was signed, our ancestors understood it to mean certain things", would certainly seem to meet the definition of hearsay. Just as the courts have categorized aboriginal title as *sui generis* (unique), however, so have

---

[50] *R. v. P. (R.)* (1990), 58 C.C.C. (3d) 334 (Ont. H.C.).

they chosen to consider the treatment of oral history without much attempt to fit it into the framework of existing evidentiary rules.

This does not mean that the courts' treatment of oral history is inconsistent with the treatment of other types of evidence. On the contrary, the pragmatic approach embodied in the contemporary application of the hearsay rule, for example, is very clearly reflected in rulings by the Supreme Court of Canada on oral history.

That a flexible approach to oral history evidence would be required was apparent in *R. v. Vanderpeet*,[51] in which Lamer C.J. stated:[52]

> . . . a court should approach the rules of evidence, and interpret the evidence that exists, with a consciousness of the special nature of aboriginal claims, and of the evidentiary difficulties in proving a right which originates in times where there were no written records of the practices, customs and traditions engaged in. The courts must not undervalue the evidence presented by aboriginal claimants simply because that evidence does not conform precisely with the evidentiary standards that would be applied in, for example, a private law torts case.

The lengths to which the Court was prepared to go to ensure that oral history evidence would not be undervalued was made very clear in *Delgamuukw*, in which the Court was sharply critical of the trial judge's application of what he understood to be the relevant principles of traditional evidence law. The court did acknowledge the difficulty in reconciling oral history evidence and traditional evidence law:[53]

> Many features of oral histories would count against both their admissibility and their weight as evidence of prior events in a court that took a traditional approach to the rules of evidence.

To the extent that evidence law might exclude oral history evidence, however, it was evidence law that would have to change:[54]

> Notwithstanding the challenges created by the use of oral histories as proof of historical facts, the laws of evidence must be adapted in order that this type of evidence can be accommodated and placed on an equal footing with the types of historical evidence that courts are familiar with, which largely consists of historical documents.

---

[51] (sub nom. *R. v. Van der Peet*) [1996] 2 S.C.R. 507 (S.C.C.).
[52] *Ibid.,* at para. 68.
[53] *Delgamuukw v. British Columbia*, [1997] 3 S.C.R. 1010 (S.C.C.) at para. 86.
[54] *Ibid.,* at para. 87.

Four years later, however, while not retreating from the approach articulated in *Delgamuukw*, the Court was expressing a note of caution:[55]

> Again, however, it must be emphasized that a consciousness of the special nature of aboriginal claims does not negate the operation of general evidentiary principles. While evidence adduced in support of aboriginal claims must not be undervalued, neither should it be interpreted or weighed in a manner that fundamentally contravenes the principles of evidence law, which, as they relate to the valuing of evidence, are often synonymous with the "general principles of common sense" (Sopinka and Lederman, *supra*, at p. 524). As Lamer C.J. emphasized in *Delgamuukw, supra*, at para. 82:
>
> > [A]boriginal rights are truly *sui generis*, and demand a unique approach to the treatment of evidence which accords due weight to the perspective of aboriginal peoples. However, that accommodation must be done in a manner which does not strain "the Canadian legal and constitutional structure" [*Van der Peet* at para. 49]. Both the principles laid down in *Van der Peet* — first, that trial courts must approach the rules of evidence in light of the evidentiary difficulties inherent in adjudicating aboriginal claims, and second, that trial courts must interpret that evidence in the same spirit — must be understood against this background. [Emphasis added.]
>
> There is a boundary that must not be crossed between a sensitive application and a complete abandonment of the rules of evidence. As Binnie J. observed in the context of treaty rights, "[g]enerous rules of interpretation should not be confused with a vague sense of after-the-fact largesse" (*R. v. Marshall*, [1999] 3 S.C.R. 456, at para. 14). In particular, the *Van der Peet* approach does not operate to amplify the cogency of evidence adduced in support of an aboriginal claim. Evidence advanced in support of aboriginal claims, like the evidence offered in any case, can run the gamut of cogency from the highly compelling to the highly dubious. Claims must still be established on the basis of persuasive evidence demonstrating their validity on the balance of probabilities. Placing "due weight" on the aboriginal perspective, or ensuring its supporting evidence an "equal footing" with more familiar forms of evidence, means precisely what these phrases suggest: equal and *due* treatment. While the evidence presented by aboriginal claimants should not be undervalued "simply because that evidence does not conform precisely with the evidentiary standards that would be applied in, for example, a private law torts case" (*Van der Peet supra*, at para. 68), neither should it be artificially strained to carry more weight than it can reasonably support. If this is an obvious proposition, it must nonetheless be stated.

After the passage of another four years, the Court was content to articulate a balanced approach to oral history evidence:[56]

---

[55] *Mitchell v. Minister of National Revenue*, (sub nom. *Mitchell v. M.N.R.*) [2001] 1 S.C.R. 911 (S.C.C.) at paras. 38-9.

[56] *R. v. Bernard*, 2005 SCC 43 (S.C.C.), at paras. 68 and 70.

Underlying all these issues is the need for a sensitive and generous approach to the evidence tendered to establish aboriginal rights, be they the right to title or lesser rights to fish, hunt or gather. Aboriginal peoples did not write down events in their pre-sovereignty histories. Therefore, orally transmitted history must be accepted, provided the conditions of usefulness and reasonable reliability set out in *Mitchell v. Minister of National Revenue*, [2001] 1 S.C.R. 911, 2001 SCC 33, are respected. Usefulness asks whether the oral history provides evidence that would not otherwise be available or evidence of the aboriginal perspective on the right claimed. Reasonable reliability ensures that the witness represents a credible source of the particular people's history. In determining the usefulness and reliability of oral histories, judges must resist facile assumptions based on Eurocentric traditions of gathering and passing on historical facts. . . .

. . .On all these matters, evidence of oral history is admissible, provided it meets the requisite standards of usefulness and reasonable reliability.

Determining whether those standards are, in fact, met may require a preliminary inquiry, similar to the qualification process for an expert witness.[57]

3. Opinion

The generally accepted rule excluding opinion evidence was noted by Major J. for the majority in *R. v. D. (D.)*:[58]

A basic tenet of our law is that the usual witness may not give opinion evidence, but testify only to facts within his knowledge, observation and experience. This is a commendable principle since it is the task of the fact finder, whether a jury or judge alone, to decide what secondary inferences are to be drawn from the facts proved.

As will be seen below, however, so broad a statement of the rule might suggest a more restrictive approach than is supported by the jurisprudence.

(a) Lay Opinion

The distinction between "fact" and "opinion" in the testimony of lay witnesses for the purpose of excluding the latter was completely

---

[57] *Xeni Gwet'in First Nations v. British Columbia*, 2004 BCSC 148 (B.C. S.C.).
[58] (2000), [2000] S.C.J. No. 44, 2000 CarswellOnt 3255, 2000 CarswellOnt 3256 (S.C.C.) at para. 49.

undermined in *R. v. Graat*,[59] a case in which two police officers were allowed to give their opinion that the ability of the accused to drive had been impaired by alcohol. After reviewing provincial and international case law, texts and law reform reports, Dickson J. for the Court began by noting the confused state of the law on opinion evidence and the recognized exceptions to the exclusion of such evidence:[60]

> We start with the reality that the law of evidence is burdened with a large number of cumbersome rules, with exclusions, and exceptions to the exclusions, and exceptions to the exceptions. The subjects upon which the non-expert witness is allowed to give opinion evidence is a lengthy one. The list mentioned in *Sherrard v. Jacob*,[61] supra, is by no means exhaustive: (i) the identification of handwriting, persons and things; (ii) apparent age; (iii) the bodily plight or condition of a person, including death and illness; (iv) the emotional state of a person—*e.g.* whether distressed, angry, aggressive, affectionate or depressed; (v) the condition of things—*e.g.* worn, shabby, used or new; (vi) certain questions of value; and (vii) estimates of speed and distance.

Rather than attempt to fit the facts of *Graat* within an existing or new exception, Dickson J. preferred to take a principled approach:[62]

> Except for the sake of convenience there is little, if any, virtue, in any distinction resting on the tenuous, and frequently false, antithesis between fact and opinion. The line between "fact" and "opinion" is not clear.
>
> To resolve the question before the Court, I would like to return to broad principles. Admissibility is determined, first, by asking whether the evidence sought to be admitted is relevant. This is a matter of applying logic and experience to the circumstances of the particular case. The question which must then be asked is whether, though probative, the evidence must be excluded by a clear ground of policy or of law.

In adopting this principled approach, Dickson J. was not deterred by two of the grounds often marshalled in support of the exclusionary approach:[63]

> As for other considerations such as "usurping the functions of the jury" and, to the extent that it may be regarded as a separate consideration, "opinion on the very issue before the jury", Wigmore has gone a long way toward establishing that rejection of opinion evidence on either of these grounds is unsound historically and in principle.

---

[59] [1982] 2 S.C.R. 819 (S.C.C.).
[60] *Ibid.*, at 835.
[61] [1965] N.I. 151 (Eng. C.A.).
[62] *Supra*, note 59, at 835.
[63] *Ibid.*, at 836.

He continued with a statement of the correct law on these points:[64]

> I agree with Professor Cross (at p. 443) that "The exclusion of opinion evidence on the ultimate issue can easily become something of a fetish". I can see no reason in principle or in common sense why a lay witness should not be permitted to testify in the form of an opinion if, by doing so, he is able more accurately to express the facts he perceived.
>
> I accept the following passage from Cross as a good statement of the law as to the cases in which non-expert opinion is admissible.
>
> When, in the words of an American judge, "the facts from which a witness received an impression were too evanescent in their nature to be recollected, or too complicated to be separately and distinctly narrated", a witness may state his opinion or impression. He was better equipped than the jury to form it, and it is impossible for him to convey an adequate idea of the premises on which he acted to the jury:
>
>> "Unless opinions, estimates and inferences which men in their daily lives reach without conscious ratiocination as a result of what they have perceived with their physical senses were treated in the law of evidence as if they were mere statements of fact, witnesses would find themselves unable to communicate to the judge an accurate impression of the events they were seeking to describe."
>
> There is nothing in the nature of a closed list of cases in which non-expert opinion evidence is admissible. Typical instances are provided by questions concerning age, speed, weather, handwriting and identity in general.

(b) Expert Opinion

The criteria by which to determine the admissibility of expert opinion evidence were re-examined in *R. v. Mohan*,[65] in which Sopinka J. for the Court stated:[66]

> Admission of expert evidence depends on the application of the following criteria:
>
> (a) relevance;
> (b) necessity in assisting the trier of fact;
> (c) the absence of any exclusionary rule;
> (d) a properly qualified expert.

---

[64] *Ibid.*, at 836-7.
[65] [1994] 2 S.C.R 9 (S.C.C.).
[66] *Ibid.*, at 20.

With regard to the first of these four criteria, relevance, Sopinka J. specified:[67]

> Relevance is a threshold requirement for the admission of expert evidence as with all other evidence. Relevance is a matter to be decided by a judge as question of law. Although *prima facie* admissible if so related to a fact in issue that it tends to establish it, that does not end the inquiry. This merely determines the logical relevance of the evidence. Other considerations enter into the decision as to admissibility. This further inquiry may be described as a cost benefit analysis, that is "whether its value is worth what it costs."

With regard to the second of the four criteria, necessity, Sopinka J. quoted from and expanded upon an earlier decision of the Court:[68]

> In *R. v. Abbey*, *supra*, Dickson J., as he then was, stated, at p. 42:
>
>> With respect to matters calling for special knowledge, an expert in the field may draw inferences and state his opinion. An expert's function is precisely this: to provide the judge and jury with a ready-made inference which the judge and jury, due to the technical nature of the facts, are unable to formulate. "An expert's opinion is admissible to furnish the Court with scientific information which is likely to be outside the experience and knowledge of a judge or jury. If on the proven facts a judge or jury can form their own conclusions without help, then the opinion of the expert is unnecessary" (Turner (1974), 60 Crim. App. R. 80, at p. 83, per Lawton L.J.)
>
> This pre-condition is often expressed in terms as to whether the evidence would be helpful to the trier of fact. The word "helpful" is not quite appropriate and sets too low a standard. However, I would not judge necessity by too strict a standard. What is required is that the opinion be necessary in the sense that it provide information "which is likely to be outside the experience and knowledge of a judge or jury": as quoted by Dickson J. in *R. v. Abbey*, *supra*. As stated by Dickson J., the evidence must be necessary to enable the trier of fact to appreciate the matters in issue due to their technical nature.

A subsequent case which shed further light on the necessity criteria was *R. v. D. (D.)*,[69] in which expert evidence regarding the interpretation to be placed upon a child's delay in reporting sex abuse was rejected as unnecessary. Major J. stated:[70]

---

[67] *Ibid.*
[68] *Ibid.*, at 23.
[69] *Supra*, note 58.
[70] *Ibid.*, at paras. 46-7.

The second requirement of the *Mohan* analysis exists to ensure that the dangers associated with expert evidence are not lightly tolerated. Mere relevance or "helpfulness" is not enough. The evidence must also be necessary.

I agree with the Chief Justice that some degree of deference is owed to the trial judge's discretionary determination of whether the *Mohan* requirements have been met on the facts of a particular case, but that discretion cannot be used erroneously to dilute the requirement of necessity. Mohan expressly states that mere helpfulness is too low a standard to warrant accepting the dangers inherent in the admission of expert evidence. *A fortiori*, a finding that some aspects of the evidence "might reasonably have assisted the jury" is not enough.

Major J. went on to adopt the following passage from Professor Paciocco:[71]

As the *Mohan* Court explained, the four-part test serves as recognition of the time and expense that is needed to cope with expert evidence. It exists in appreciation of the distracting and time-consuming thing that expert testimony can become. It reflects the realization that simple humility and a desire to do what is right can tempt triers of fact to defer to what the expert says. It even addresses the fact that with expert testimony, lawyers may be hard-pressed to perform effectively their function of probing and testing and challenging evidence because its subject matter will often pull them beyond their competence, let alone their expertise. This leaves the trier of fact without sufficient information to assess its reliability adequately, increasing the risk that the expert opinion will simply be attorned to. When should we place the legal system and the truth at such risk by allowing expert evidence? Only when lay persons are apt to come to a wrong conclusion without expert assistance, or where access to important information will be lost unless we borrow from the learning of experts. As *Mohan* tells us, it is not enough that the expert evidence be helpful before we will be prepared to run these risks. That sets too low a standard. It must be necessary.

As an example of the third of the four criteria, the absence of any exclusionary rule, Sopinka J. in *Mohan* gave the example of *R. v. Morin*,[72] in which evidence elicited by the Crown in cross-examination of the psychiatrist called by the accused was inadmissible because it was not shown to be relevant other than as to the disposition to commit the crime charged. Admission of the evidence in that case would have violated the rule against character evidence where character has not already been put in issue by the accused.

---

[71] Paciocco, David. "Expert Evidence: Where Are We Now? Where Are We Going?". Institute of Continuing Legal Education, Canadian Bar Association (Ontario), January 31, 1998.

[72] [1988] 2 S.C.R. 345 (S.C.C.).

Regarding the fourth criterion, a properly qualified expert, Sopinka J. simply said:[73]

> Finally the evidence must be given by a witness who is shown to have acquired special or peculiar knowledge through study or experience in respect of the matters on which he or she undertakes to testify.

What constitutes a properly qualified expert is, of course, almost invariably a disputatious matter. In addition, there is always the danger that an expert who may be properly qualified to give evidence in a particular field will give opinions that are outside of that field of qualification; when this occurs, the evidence must be given no weight.[74]

(c) Opinion on the Ultimate Issue

The quotes in the preceding section on lay opinion evidence regarding the "ultimate issue" might give the impression that the Supreme Court of Canada had considered this issue and — as with other subfields of evidence law — clarified it through the adoption of a principled approach. Such an impression would be inaccurate, since courts continue to issue inconsistent judgments regarding this subject.

The fact that courts do allow opinion evidence to be adduced despite claims that it infringes the ultimate issue rule indicates, at least, that this can no longer be a very strict rule. As stated by McLachlin J. in *R. v. B. (R.H.)*[75] with regard to psychiatric evidence bearing on a witness' behaviour:[76]

> His objection is that "the opinion of Dr. Maddess went to the very root of the issue before the learned trial judge" and that "allowing that opinion usurped the function of the trial judge": the so-called "ultimate issue rule". However, the jurisprudence does not support such a strict application of this rule. While care must be taken to ensure that the judge or jury, and not the expert, makes the final decisions on all issues in the case, it has long been accepted that expert evidence on matters of fact should not be excluded simply because it suggests answers to issues which are at the core of the dispute before the court: . . .

---

[73] *Mohan, supra.*, note 65 at 25.

[74] *L. (H.) v. Canada (Attorney General)*, 2005 SCC 25 (S.C.C.) at paras. 315-7.

[75] [1994] 1 S.C.R. 656 (S.C.C.).

[76] *Ibid.*, at para. 25.

In the same year, Sopinka J. in *R. v. Mohan*[77] indicated that although the rule might no longer be an absolute one, it was not completely without effect:[78]

> These concerns were the basis of the rule which excluded expert evidence in respect of the ultimate issue. Although the rule is no longer of general application, the concerns underlying it remain. In light of these concerns, the criteria of relevance and necessity are applied strictly, on occasion, to exclude expert evidence as to an ultimate issue. Expert evidence as to credibility or oath-helping has been excluded on this basis.

Does this mean that opinion evidence is no longer excluded simply for being too close to the ultimate issue? In practice, no. See, for example, the decision in *Thiessen v. Columbia Shuswap (Regional District)*,[79] in which the evidence of a well-qualified engineer with particular expertise in the design and evaluation of landfill and transfer stations was rejected:[80]

> Mr. Thiessen objects to the introduction of Dr. Cameron's opinion claiming that it usurps the function of the court by stating an opinion on the ultimate issue before the court, that is, whether the safety features of the Columbia Shuswap Regional District Transfer Station were reasonable considering all of the complexities of safety feature design for transfer stations. I agree with that submission. That is an issue to be resolved by the court.

Perhaps the most accurate statement of the current approach is an extrapolation that some courts[81] have made from a statement in the reasons of Sopinka J. in *Mohan*.[82] Specifically with respect to novel scientific evidence, he had written that it was subject to special scrutiny to see whether it met standards for necessity and reliability, and that the closer it came to the ultimate issue, the more strictly *that* principle would be applied. Some courts, however, have interpreted this as meaning that the closer opinion evidence gets to the ultimate issue, the more strictly the ultimate issue rule will be applied. Even if this misconstrues what Sopinka J. said, the result is a not illogical one.

---

[77] [1994] 2 S.C.R. 9 (S.C.C.).

[78] *Ibid.,* at para. 25.

[79] (2002), [2002] B.C.J. No. 2482, 2002 CarswellBC 2637 (B.C. S.C.), affirmed (2003), 2 M.P.L.R. (4th) 83 (B.C. C.A.), leave to appeal refused (2004), 330 N.R. 393 (note) (S.C.C.).

[80] *Ibid.,* at [CarswellBC] para 24.

[81] *Lunenburg Industrial Foundry & Engineering Ltd. v. Commercial Union Assurance Co. of Canada* (2004), [2004] N.S.J. No. 525, 2004 CarswellNS 574 (N.S. S.C.) at paras. 27-9.

[82] *Supra,* at para. 25.

4. Privilege

(a) The General Principle

In *M. (A.) v. Ryan*,[83] a case dealing with the production of a psychiatrist's notes from the counselling of the plaintiff sexual assault victim, McLachlin J. for the majority said:[84]

> The common law principles underlying the recognition of privilege from disclosure are simply stated. They proceed from the fundamental proposition that everyone owes a general duty to give evidence relevant to the matter before the court, so that the truth may be ascertained. To this fundamental duty, the law permits certain exceptions, known as privileges, where it can be shown that they are required by a "public good transcending the normally predominant principle of utilizing all rational means for ascertaining truth": *Trammel v. United States*, 445 U.S. 40 (1980), at p. 50.

(b) Privilege Is Not Like Other Exclusionary Rules

The distinction between the exclusion of evidence on the grounds of privilege and the exclusion of evidence on other grounds was noted by the Quebec Court of Appeal in *Ciments Canada Lafarge Ltée v. Société d'énergie de la Baie James*:[85]

> *Sopinka et Lederman, The Law of Evidence in civil Cases, Butterworths & Co., Toronto, 1974, page 156, expliquent la raison d'être d'un tel privilège de confidentialité des communications des parties visant au règlement des litiges et les inconvénients de la règle:*
>
> Page 156:
>
> "At the outset, a distinction must be drawn between evidence which is excluded by reason of incompetency and evidence excluded because of privilege. Hearsay, opinion and character evidence, as a general rule, are excluded because of their inherent unreliability, lack of probative worth and susceptibility to fabrication. These are all dangers related to the adversary method of ascertaining the truth. Moreover, in order to minimize the risk of the trier of fact, in his search for truth, relying on untested and untrustworthy proof, such evidence is excluded from the fact-finding process. The exclu-

---

[83] [1997] 1 S.C.R. 157 (S.C.C.).
[84] *Ibid.*, at 170.
[85] (1991), (sub nom. *Lafarge Canada Inc. c. Société d'énergie de la Baie James*) 37 Q.A.C. 241 (Que. C.A.) at 250, per Dugas J.A. (*ad hoc*).

sionary rule of privilege, however, rests upon a different foundation. It is based upon social values, external to the trial process.

Although such evidence is relevant, probative and trustworthy, and would thus advance the just resolution of disputes, it is excluded because of over-riding social interests. Thus, in recognizing the exclusionary rule of privilege, the courts have been prepared to sacrifice, in some measure, their ability to inquire into all material facts, in order to preserve a societal interest in non-disclosure."

Page 157:

"The extension of the doctrine of privilege consequentially obstructs the truth-finding process, and, accordingly, the law has been reluctant to prolif-erate the areas of privilege unless an external social policy is demonstrated to be of such unequivocal importance that it demands protection."

(c) Privilege Belongs to the Client and Can Be Waived By the Client

In *Goodman Estate v. Geffen*,[86] a case which involved a solicitor's evidence as to whether the deceased had been subject to undue influence, Wilson J. noted:[87]

Thus, while at one time it was thought that the privilege belonged to the solicitor and not to his client, there is now no doubt that the privilege belongs to the client alone. One consequence of this is that confidential communications between solicitor and client can only be divulged in certain circumscribed situations. The client may, of course, herself choose to disclose the contents of her communica-tions with her legal representative and thereby waive the privilege. Or, the client may authorize the solicitor to reveal those communications for her. Even then, however, the courts have been cautious in allowing such disclosures, so much so that they have assumed for themselves the role of ensuring that without the client's express consent a solicitor may not testify.

(d) Two Kinds of Privilege

In *R. v. Fosty*,[88] Lamer J. analyzed the distinction between two types of privilege:[89]

---

[86] (sub nom. *Geffen v. Goodman Estate*) [1991] 2 S.C.R. 353 (S.C.C.).

[87] *Ibid.*, at 383.

[88] (sub nom. *R. v. Gruenke*) [1991] 3 S.C.R. 263 (S.C.C.).

[89] *Ibid.*, at 286.

Before delving into an analysis of the issues raised by this appeal, I think it is important to clarify the terminology being used in this case. The parties have tended to distinguish between two categories: a "blanket", *prima facie*, common law, or "class" privilege on the one hand, and a "case-by-case" privilege on the other. The first four terms are used to refer to a privilege which was recognized at common law and one for which there is a *prima facie* presumption of inadmissibility (once it has been established that the relationship fits within the class) unless the party urging admission can show why the communications should not be privileged (*i.e.* why they should be admitted into evidence as an exception to the general rule). Such communications are excluded not because the evidence is not relevant, but rather because, there are overriding policy reasons to exclude this relevant evidence. Solicitor-client communications appear to fall within this first category....The term "case-by-case" privilege is used to refer to communications for which there is a *prima facie* assumption that they are not privileged (*i.e.*, are admissible). The case-by-case analysis has generally involved an application of the "Wigmore test" (see above), which is a set of criteria for determining whether communications should be privileged (and therefore not admitted) in particular cases. In other words, the case-by-case analysis requires that the policy reasons for excluding otherwise relevant evidence be weighed in each particular case.

The four criteria of the "Wigmore test" were set out at p. 284:

(1) The communications must originate in a *confidence* that they will not be disclosed.
(2) This element of *confidentiality must be essential* to the full and satisfactory maintenance of the relation between the parties.
(3) The *relation* must be one which in the opinion of the community ought to be sedulously *fostered*.
(4) The *injury* that would inure to the relation by the disclosure of the communications must be *greater than the benefit* thereby gained for the correct disposal of litigation.

(e) Onus of Establishing Privilege

With regard to solicitor-client privilege, Cory J. in *Smith v. Jones*[90] stated:[91]

It is because of the fundamental importance of the privilege that the onus properly rests upon those seeking to set aside the privilege to justify taking such a significant step.

---

[90] [1999] 1 S.C.R. 455 (S.C.C.).
[91] *Ibid.*, at 475.

With regard to privilege asserted on a case-by-case basis, however, it would appear that the party asserting the privilege has the onus of establishing its existence:[92]

> It is a qualified form of privilege and four fundamental conditions as outlined by Wigmore on Evidence, (3rd Ed.) Vol. 8 are necessary to establish the privilege successfully. There is no blanket acknowledgment of the privilege, rather it has to be granted, if at all, on a case by case basis — *R. v. Gruenke* (1991), 67 C.C.C. (3d) 289. And it is the claimant who has the burden of establishing that the communication should be excluded.

(f) Is Privilege An All-Or-Nothing Proposition?

With regard to psychiatric records, the Supreme Court of Canada in *M. (A.) v. Ryan*[93] rejected an all-or-nothing approach to disclosure:[94]

> It follows that if the court considering a claim for privilege determines that a particular document or class of documents must be produced to get at the truth and prevent an unjust verdict, it must permit production to the extent required to avoid that result. On the other hand, the need to get at the truth and avoid injustice does not automatically negate the possibility of protection from full disclosure. In some cases, the court may well decide that the truth permits of nothing less than full production. This said, I would venture to say that an order for partial privilege will more often be appropriate in civil cases where, as here, the privacy interest is compelling. Disclosure of a limited number of documents, editing by the court to remove non-essential material, and the imposition of conditions on who may see and copy the documents are techniques which may be used to ensure the highest degree of confidentiality and the least damage to the protected relationship, while guarding against the injustice of cloaking the truth.
>
> In taking this approach, I respectfully decline to follow the all-or-nothing approach adopted by the majority of the Supreme Court of the United States of endorsing an absolute privilege for all psychotherapeutic records in *Jaffee v. Redmond, supra*.

---

[92] *R. v. Mirkhandan* (1999), [1999] O.J. No. 3215, 1999 CarswellOnt 2674 (Ont. C.J.).

[93] [1997] 1 S.C.R. 157.

[94] *Ibid.*, at 177.

(g) What is the Procedure For Ascertaining Privilege In Cases Where Partial Privilege May Be Appropriate?

In *M. (A.) v. Ryan*, McLachlin J. for the majority explicitly spelled out the procedure to be followed regarding — in that case — psychiatric records:[95]

> In order to determine whether privilege should be accorded to a particular document or class of documents and, if so, what conditions should attach, the judge must consider the circumstances of the privilege alleged, the documents and the case. While it is not essential in a civil case such as this that the judge examine every document, the court may do so if necessary to the inquiry. On the other hand, a judge does not necessarily err by proceeding on affidavit material indicating the nature of the information and its expected relevance without inspecting each document individually. The requirement that the Court minutely examine numerous or lengthy documents may prove time-consuming, expensive and delay the resolution of the litigation. Where necessary to the proper determination of the claim for privilege, it must be undertaken. But I would not lay down an absolute rule that as a matter of law, the judge must personally inspect every document at issue in every case. Where the judge is satisfied on reasonable grounds that the interests at stake can properly be balanced without individual examination of each document, failure to do so does not constitute error of law.

(h) Solicitor-Client

The general principles of solicitor-client privilege were explicated by Dickson J. in *Solosky v. Canada*:[96]

> The concept of privileged communications between a solicitor and his client has long been recognized as fundamental to the due administration of justice. As Jackett C.J. aptly stated in *Re Director of Investigation and Research and Shell Canada Ltd.* [(1975), 22 C.C.C. (2d) 70, [1975] F.C. 184], at pp. 78-9:
>
> > ... the protection, civil and criminal, afforded to the individual by our law is dependent upon his having the aid and guidance of those skilled in the law untrammelled by any apprehension that the full and frank disclosure by him of all his facts and thoughts to his legal advisor might somehow become available to third persons so as to be used against him.
>
> The history of the privilege can be traced to the reign of Elizabeth I (see *Berd v. Lovelace* [(1577), 21 E.R. 33] and *Dennis v. Codrington* [(1580), 21 E.R. 53]). It stemmed from respect for the 'oath and honour' of the lawyer, dutybound to

[95] *Ibid.*, at 180.
[96] (1979), (sub nom. *Solosky v. R.*) [1980] 1 S.C.R. 821 (S.C.C.) at 833-6.

guard closely the secrets of his client, and was restricted in operation to an exemption from testimonial compulsion. Thereafter, in stages, privilege was extended to include communications exchanged during other litigation, those made in contemplation of litigation, and finally, any consultation for legal advice, whether litigious or not. The classic statement of the policy grounding the privilege was given by Brougham L.C. in *Greenough v. Gaskell* [(1833), 39 E.R. 618], at p. 620:

> The foundation of this rule is not difficult to discover. It is not (as has sometimes been said) on account of any particular importance which the law attributes to the business of legal professors, or any particular disposition to afford them protection (though certainly it may not be very easy to discover why a like privilege has been refused to others, and especially to medical advisers).

> But it is out of regard to the interests of justice, which cannot be upholden, and to the administration of justice, which cannot go on without the aid of men skilled in jurisprudence, in the practice of the courts, and in those matters affecting rights and obligations which form the subject of all judicial proceedings. If the privilege did not exist at all, every one would be thrown upon his own legal resources. Deprived of all professional assistance, a man would not venture to consult any skilful person, or would only dare to tell his counsellor half his case.

The rationale was put this way by Jessel M.R. in *Anderson v. Bank of British Columbia* [(1876), 2 Ch. D. 644], at p. 649:

> The object and meaning of the rule is this: that as, by reason of the complexity and difficulty of our law, litigation can only be properly conducted by professional men, it is absolutely necessary that a man, in order to prosecute his rights or to defend himself from an improper claim, should have resource to the assistance of professional lawyers, and it being so absolutely necessary, it is equally necessary, to use a vulgar phrase, that he should be able to make a clean breast of it to the gentleman whom he consults with a view to the prosecution of his claim, or the substantiating of his defence against the claim of others; that he should be able to place unrestricted and unbounded confidence in the professional agent, and that the communications he so makes to him should be kept secret, unless with his consent (for it is his privilege, and not the privilege of the confidential agent), that he should be enabled properly to conduct his litigation.

Wigmore [8 Wigmore, Evidence (McNaughton rev. 1961) para. 2292] framed the modern principle of privilege for solicitor-client communications, as follows:

> Where legal advice of any kind is sought from a professional legal adviser in his capacity as such, the communications relating to the purpose made in confidence by the client are at his instance permanently protected from

disclosures by himself or by the legal adviser, except the protection be waived.

> There are exceptions to the privilege. The privilege does not apply to communications in which legal advice is neither sought nor offered, that is to say, where the lawyer is not contacted in his professional capacity. Also, where the communication is not intended to be confidential, privilege will not attach, *O'Shea* v. *Wood* [[1891] P. 286], at p. 289. More significantly, if a client seeks guidance from a lawyer in order to facilitate the commission of a crime or a fraud, the communication will not be privileged and it is immaterial whether the lawyer is an unwitting dupe or knowing participant. The classic case is *R. v. Cox and Railton* [(1884), 14 Q.B.D. 153], in which Stephen J. had this to say (p. 167): "A communication in furtherance of a criminal purpose does not 'come in the ordinary scope of professional employment'."

Although solicitor-client privilege is not absolute, "the occasions when the solicitor-client privilege yields are rare and the test to be met is a stringent one."[97] Not only will legislation purporting to limit or deny solicitor-client privilege be interpreted restrictively, but it is "a controversial matter" even whether solicitor-client privilege can be violated by the express intention of the legislature.[98]

(i) Clergy

In *R. v. Fosty*,[99] Lamer C.J. for the majority ruled with regard to conflicting arguments about the existence of a privilege for religious communications:[100]

> While the appellant may well be correct in pointing out that English and Canadian courts have not, as a matter of <u>practice</u>, compelled members of the clergy to disclose confidential religious communications, this does not answer the question of whether there is a <u>legal</u> common law privilege for religious communications. Furthermore, I cannot agree with the appellant that the existence of a limited statutory religious privilege in some jurisdictions (see: Quebec's *Charter of Human Rights and Freedoms*, R.S.Q., c. C-12, s. 9, and Newfoundland's *Evidence Act*, R.S.N. 1970, c. 115, s. 6) indicates that a common law privilege exists. If anything, the fact that there is a statutory privilege in some jurisdictions indicates that the common law did not protect religious communications — thus necessitating the statutory protection.

---

[97] *R. v. McClure* (2001), [2001] S.C.J. No. 13, 2001 CarswellOnt 496 (S.C.C.) at para. 5, per Major J. for the Court.

[98] *Pritchard v. Ontario (Human Rights Commission)*, [2004] 1 S.C.R. 809 (S.C.C.) at paras. 33-4.

[99] (sub nom. *R. v. Gruenke*) [1991] 3 S.C.R. 263 (S.C.C.).

[100] *Ibid.* at 287-8.

In considering first whether a class privilege similar to that for solicitor-client communications existed, Lamer C.J. went on to find:[101]

> In my view, the policy reasons which underlay the treatment of solicitor-client communications as a separate class from most other confidential communications, are not equally applicable to religious communications.

The court therefore went on to consider privilege in that case on the basis of applying Wigmore's four principles to a case-by-case analysis.

(j) Doctors and Counsellors

That communications with doctors, psychologists, psychiatrists and other counsellors were not subject to a common law privilege was noted explicitly by Lampkin J. in *R. v. Mirkhandan*:[102]

> The claim of privilege of communications between a doctor and his patient or a counsellor and his client is to be approached on a case by case basis. These communications are not of the high quality of a "class" privilege.

The Supreme Court of Canada has utilized a case-by-case analysis in these situations in cases such as *M.(A.) v. Ryan*[103] and *A. (L.L) v. B. (A.)*.[104]

With regard to medical therapist records, the Court has noted that a different rule applies:[105]

> Medical therapist records are different because, although a traditional common law privilege does not attach to these documents, a right to confidentiality exists upon balancing individual rights: the reasonable expectation of privacy of the third person versus the right to make full answer and defence to a criminal charge. The procedure for protection of such records is codified in ss. 278.1 to 278.9 of the Criminal Code, R.S.C. 1985, c. C-46.

5. Self-Serving Evidence

The exclusionary rule against the admission of self-serving evidence has more than one aspect. In *R. v. Béland*,[106] McIntyre J. for the majority considered the question of whether the defendants might be

---

[101] *Ibid.* at 288-9.
[102] (1999), [1999] O.J. No. 3215, 1999 CarswellOnt 2674 (Ont. C.J.) at [CarswellOnt] para. 24.
[103] [1997] 1 S.C.R. 157 (S.C.C.).
[104] [1995] 4 S.C.R. 536 (S.C.C.).
[105] *R. v. McClure*, [2001] 1 S.C.R. 445 (S.C.C.) at 456.
[106] [1987] 2 S.C.R. 398 (S.C.C.).

able to voluntarily submit to polygraph examinations. He discussed the rule against "oath-helping" — *i.e.* evidence of the good character of a witness — the rule against evidence of prior consistent statements, and the rule as it relates to expert evidence:[107]

> The Crown appellant argues that the admission of polygraph evidence offends the rule which prohibits a party from presenting evidence which has, as its sole purpose, the bolstering of the credibility of that party's own witnesses. This is sometimes referred to in the earlier cases as oath-helping.

The Court cited with approval the decision in *R. v. Kyselka*,[108] which was referred to as the "leading decision on this point in Canada". In that case, which involved psychiatric testimony that a mentally retarded girl lacked sufficient imagination to have fabricated her rape complaint, Porter C.J.O. said:[109]

> While the credit of any witness may be *impeached* by the *opposite party*, *R. v. Gunewardene*, [1951] 2 All E.R. 290 at p. 294, there is no warrant or authority for such oath-helping as occurred in the circumstances of this case, reminiscent as it is of the method before the Norman Conquest by which a defendant in a civil suit or an accused person proved his case by calling witnesses to swear that the oath of the party was true. If this sort of evidence were admissible in the case of either party no limit could be placed on the number of witnesses who could be called to testify about the credibility of witnesses as to facts. It would tend to produce, regardless of the number of such character witnesses who were called, undue confusion in the minds of the jury by directing their attention away from the real issues and the controversy would become so intricate that truth would be more likely to remain hidden than be discovered. For these reasons this evidence was not admissible.

(a) Prior Consistent Statements

McIntyre J. stated the following with regard to prior consistent statements:[110]

> The rule against oath-helping is also consistent in principle with other rules of evidence which in some degree may be said to overlap it and which are based on similar principles. An example is the rule against the admission of previous consistent statements of a witness. McWilliams, *supra*, discusses this rule, at p. 353, and refers to the frequently quoted words of Neville J. in *Jones v. South-Eastern and Chatham Railway* (1917), 87 L.J.K.B. 775 (C.A.), at p. 779, that:

---

[107] *Ibid.*, at 404-5.
[108] (1962), 133 C.C.C. 103 (Ont. C.A.).
[109] *Ibid.* at 107.
[110] In *Béland, supra,* note 106 at 409.

... statements may be used against a witness as admissions, but... you are not entitled to give evidence of statements on other occasions by the witness in confirmation of her testimony.

This was said in the context of a case where an injury was alleged to have been suffered by the plaintiff while at her work, and it was sought to adduce evidence of a statement she had made after the accident to a third party. McWilliams also cites *R. v. Campbell* (1977), 38 C.C.C. (2d) 6 (Ont. C.A.), where Martin J.A., speaking for the court (Arnup, Martin and Lacourcière JJ.A.), said, at p. 18:

The refusal of the trial Judge to admit the evidence of other witnesses, whether in cross-examination or otherwise, of previous statements made by the appellant, involves two separate rules of evidence:
I. The rule which precludes an accused from eliciting from witnesses self-serving statements which he has previously made.
II. The rule which provides that a witness, whether a party or not, may not repeat his own previous statements concerning the matter before the Court, made to other persons out of Court, and may not call other persons to testify to those statements.
Statements made by an accused which infringe rule I are excluded as hearsay. The narration by a witness of earlier statements made to other persons out of Court appears to be excluded under rule II, because of the general lack of probative value of such evidence, save in certain circumstances, in support of the credibility of the witness.

Wigmore, *supra*, at p. 255, para. 1124, describes the rule in these terms:

When the witness has merely testified on direct examination, without any impeachment, proof of consistent statements is unnecessary and valueless. The witness is not helped by it; for, even if it is an improbable or untrustworthy story, it is not made more probable or more trustworthy by any number of repetitions of it. Such evidence would ordinarily be cumbersome to the trial and is ordinarily rejected.

(b) Exceptions That Allow Self-Serving Evidence

The rule against the admission of prior consistent statements and other self-serving evidence admits of some exceptions, as noted by McIntyre J. for the Court in *R. v. Simpson*:[111]

As a general rule, the statements of an accused person made outside court — subject to a finding of voluntariness where the statement is made to one in authority — are receivable in evidence against him but not for him. This rule is based on the sound proposition that an accused person should not be free to make

---

[111] [1988] 1 S.C.R. 3 (S.C.C.) at 22.

an unsworn statement and compel its admission into evidence through other witnesses and thus put his defence before the jury without being put on oath and being subjected, as well, to cross-examination. It is, however, not an inflexible rule, and in proper circumstances such statements may be admissible; for example, where they are relevant to show the state of mind of an accused at a given time or to rebut the suggestion of recent fabrication of a defence.

(i) Recent Fabrication

In *Simpson*, the Court also accepted that the exception to rebut the suggestion of recent fabrication of a defence would not arise only where that suggestion was made explicitly:[112]

> The courts have recently applied this exception to the general rule against the admission of self-serving statements by the accused where no direct allegation of recent fabrication has been made. In *R. v. Giraldi* (1975), 28 C.C.C. (2d) 248 (B.C. C.A.), McFarlane J.A., speaking for the court (McFarlane, Branca, Carrothers JJ.A.), said, at p. 253:
>
> > I find the reasoning of the Judges in this case impelling. That reasoning does not support the proposition that the only basis for applying the exception and admitting the evidence is the fact that cross-examination of the witness has been of such a nature as to lay a foundation for inferring a recently fabricated or contrived story. On the contrary it supports the view, which in my opinion is the correct one, that that foundation may be laid in other ways including the whole circumstances of the case and the conduct of the trial. Moreover, it is very much a matter for the trial Judge who is required to consider the question of admissibility with great care before allowing the earlier self-serving statement to be admitted.
> >
> > I think also this view that a suggestion of recent fabrication need not necessarily be made expressly but may arise implicitly is supported on a careful consideration of the judgments of the Ontario Court of Appeal in *R. v. Pappin* (1970), 12 C.R.N.S. 287, and *R. v. Rosik* (1970), 2 C.C.C. (2d) 351, [1971] 2 O.R. 47, 13 C.R.N.S. 129 (appeal in the latter to the Supreme Court of Canada dismissed, 2 C.C.C. (2d) 393n, [1971] 2 O.R. 89n, [1971] S.C.R. vi).
>
> And in *R. v. Campbell* (1977), 38 C.C.C. (2d) 6 (Ont. C.A.), Martin J.A., speaking for the court (Arnup, Martin and Lacourcière JJ.A.), said, at pp. 18-19:
>
> > I accept the proposition that an express allegation of recent fabrication in cross-examination is not necessary before the exception with respect to rebutting an allegation of recent fabrication becomes operative, and that a

---

[112] *Ibid.*, at 24.

suggestion that the accused's story has been recently contrived may also arise implicitly from the whole circumstances of the case, the evidence of the witnesses who have been called, and the conduct of the trial. Where the circumstances are such as to raise the suggestion that the accused's evidence is a recent fabrication, counsel may properly anticipate the allegation of recent fabrication in cross-examination, and examine the accused in chief with respect to previous statements to other persons, prior to his being cross-examined: see *R. v. Giraldi* (1975), 28 C.C.C. (2d) 248, [1975] W.W.D. 166; *R. v. Racine* (1977), 32 C.C.C. (2d) 468, at p. 473; *Previous Consistent Statements*, at pp. 86-7, by R.N. Gooderson.

From these authorities, it is my view that the second statement made by Simpson could in proper circumstances have been admitted in evidence at the request of Simpson.

(ii) Sexual Assault

Another exception to the rule is to prove "recent complaint" in sexual assault cases, an exception which became less important with the introduction of s. 275 of the *Criminal Code*. This exception was discussed by Lamer J. for the Court in *R. v. Timm*,[113] in which he held that the exception is not limited to cases where the prior statement was explicit with regard to sexual assault having occurred:

That the trier of fact may be apprised of complaints made by the alleged victim of a sexual offence is an exception to the rule at common law that a witness' testimony-in-chief may not be buttressed by the party calling her by proving that she has made a prior consistent statement (by asking her or otherwise).

That exception was recognized as necessary to negate the adverse effect the alleged victim's silence might have on her credibility when relating the circumstances of the offence and, if essential to the commission of the offence or simply averred by the victim, the victim's credibility when asserting absence of consent. (*R. v. Lillyman, supra*; *R. v. Osborne, supra*; *Thomas v. The Queen* [[1952] 2 S.C.R. 344], at p. 355). That possible adverse effect is predicated upon the assumption that the true victim of a sexual offence will, under normal circumstances, complain at the first reasonable opportunity. Early complaint evidence seeks to negate the inference that could otherwise be drawn from the victim's silence as a result of that assumption.

This negation being the purpose and that assumption being the justification of the exception to the general rule, one can then logically conclude that the exception should operate whenever the victim's silence might have, given the nature of the offence and the circumstances of that particular case, an adverse effect on her

---

[113] [1981] 2 S.C.R. 315 (S.C.C.) at 321-3.

credibility, and if the victim's complaint is of such a nature and was made under such circumstances as to be of some probative value in rebutting that adverse effect. Though the rule was extended to all types of sexual offences and to both sexes, an indiscriminate recognition of the assumption does not appear to have been questioned and any victim's silence is of relevance as regards her credibility. Be that as it may, this case is one of rape where consent is in issue, and we therefore need not consider whether the relevancy of a victim's silence, and as a corollary that of a victim's departure from same, can ever be in question, for it undoubtedly will always be relevant in this type of case.

What then is to be determined on a *voir dire* in a rape case is whether there was a complaint that is of such a nature and made under such circumstances as to be of some probative value in negating beforehand in some way the adverse effect the victim's silence would have on her credibility as a result of that assumption.

The precise purpose for admitting such evidence, while limiting its use (it is not proof of the facts nor is it corroboration evidence), in turn suggests, in my opinion, a wide definition of what is to be considered a complaint. In my view, any statement made by the alleged victim, which is of some probative value in negating the adverse conclusions the jury might be invited to make and could draw as regards her credibility had she remained silent, is to be considered a complaint. It will have the effect of negating that adverse conclusion if it is in some way supportive of the victim's credibility by showing consistency between the victim's conduct after the alleged ravishment and the victim's narration of same as a witness.

Because it is supportive of the witness' testimony to the effect that she was the victim of a sexual crime, we refer to it as being a "sexual complaint" or "a complaint of rape ..." This is not to say however, as some courts have held, that it must be a complaint that directly alleges a sexual attack; I think it sufficient that the early statement made by the alleged victim be in some way useful to the trier of fact in restricting, if not wholly negating, the adverse effect total silence would have had on the victim's credibility.

The all or nothing approach, that is letting in only complaints that refer to a sexual assault, is hard to reconcile with the very purpose of the rule, the rebuttal of the inference that silence suggests as a result of the assumption. If silence, given the nature and circumstances of the case considered, is to be of some probative value adverse to the victim, then, subject to the other requirements of the rule and of the other rules of evidence, any departure from silence is relevant and admissible. It will either help the Crown or the defence, but will always, in such a case, serve the jury in weighing the victim's credibility.

(iii) Res Gestae

In *R. v. F. (J.E.)*,[114] Finlayson J.A. described the *res gestae* exception and expressed reservation about it:[115]

> This is a phrase used in the law of evidence to explain the admissibility of words used by a person that shed light upon the quality of the act they accompany. The words are considered to be so interrelated to a fact in issue that they become a part of the fact itself. To qualify, the words must introduce the fact in issue, explain its nature, or form in connection with it one continuous transaction: see Jowitt's, *ibid.* I do not regard *res gestae* as a fertile area for enlarging the admissibility of prior consistent statements.

An example of the recognition of this principle by the Supreme Court of Canada is *R. v. Graham*,[116] in which Ritchie J. noted with regard to a statement by an accused at the time of arrest that he had never seen a briefcase full of stolen jewellery before in his life:[117]

> In the present case the respondent's verbal statement made when the attaché case was found, that he had never seen it before in his life, being one which was immediately connected with the initial discovery of the stolen goods, was properly admitted in evidence. Explanatory statements made by an accused upon his first being found "in possession" constitute a part of the *res gestae* and are necessarily admissible in any description of the circumstances under which the crime was committed....

In *R. v. Khan*,[118] McLachlin J. noted that the time within which statements can be considered to constitute part of the *res gestae* may *be* flexible in some circumstances:[119]

> Similarly, Wharton's *Criminal Evidence* (13th ed. 1972), at p. 84, states that while "[t]he *res gestae* rule in sex crimes is the same as in other criminal actions", the rule "should be applied more liberally in the case of children". In an attempt to analyze the many authorities in this area and arrive at some general "rule of thumb" with respect to the generally permissible time lapse between the alleged sexual assault and the spontaneous declaration, the author notes that declarations made up to an hour following the assault will generally be admissible, whereas such declarations "will not ordinarily be regarded as part of the res gestae where the time interval between the crime and the declaration is more than one hour" (p. 90).

---

[114] (1993), 85 C.C.C. (3d) 457 (Ont. C.A.).
[115] *Ibid.*, at 470.
[116] (1972), [1974] S.C.R. 206 (S.C.C.).
[117] *Ibid.*, at 213-4.
[118] [1990] 2 S.C.R. 531 (S.C.C.).
[119] *Ibid.*, at 543.

(c) Videotaped Evidence of Children

The admission of the videotaped evidence of child complainants in sexual assault cases pursuant to s. 715.1 of the *Criminal Code* might at first appear to be an exception to the rule against prior consistent statements, given that there is no opportunity for cross-examination at the time the statement is taken, and the complainant at trial adopts the statement given earlier. L'Heureux Dubé J. dismissed this argument in *R. v. L. (D.O.):*[120]

> The respondent's second line of attack on the constitutionality of s. 715.1 of the Criminal Code is that the admission of prior consistent statements violates the fundamental principles of justice. The general evidentiary rule with regard to the admission of prior consistent statements is expressed by Wigmore:
>
> > When the witness has merely testified on direct examination, without any impeachment, proof of consistent statements is unnecessary and valueless. The witness is not helped by it; for, even if it is an improbable or untrustworthy story, it is not made more probable or more trustworthy by any number of repetitions of it. Such evidence would ordinarily be cumbersome to the trial and is ordinarily rejected.
>
> > (*Wigmore on Evidence*, vol. 4 (Chadbourn rev. 1972), (SS) 1124, at p. 255.)
>
> In my opinion, the above rationale for excluding prior consistent statements made by a witness is not applicable to s. 715.1 of the *Criminal Code*. This Court has dealt at length with evidentiary concerns, and the potential violation of an accused's rights in this regard, in *Seaboyer, supra,* and, most recently, with respect to videotaped testimony in *B. (K.G.), supra.*
>
> Although the admittance of a prior consistent statement would, perhaps, be considered an exception to the general rule, the facts of this case are quite different from situations regularly caught by the rule against prior consistent statements. As a result of s. 715.1 of the *Criminal Code*, the prior consistent statement is not being admitted to bolster the credibility of the child witness or to provide superfluous information. The videotaped evidence is the only evidence before the court with regard to the details of the child's sexual abuse. It is, in fact, the evidence itself, as if the child were giving it in open court or in lieu of open court evidence. Thus, I agree with the appellant that the videotaped evidence is highly relevant and probative and is neither "unnecessary [or] valueless". Section 715.1 of the *Code* simply provides a different means of giving evidence. In that sense, it cannot even be said that it affords an exception to the rule against the admissibility of prior consistent statements, the rationale of which does not apply in this case.

---

[120] [1993] 4 S.C.R. 419 (S.C.C.) at 457-8.

Although the Court draws a neat distinction and says that the rule against prior consistent statements simply does not apply in the case of s. 715.1, the Court's willingness to consider the underlying rationale of the rule suggests that this is another example of the move away from the strict application of the old, exclusionary rules to a policy-based approach.

6. Confessions

The common law rule on confessions and its relationship to the *Charter* was thoroughly canvassed in *R. v. Oickle*,[121] a case in which an accused, although having been cautioned as to his *Charter* rights, confessed under extremely skilful police interrogation to a series of arsons. Iacobucci J. for the majority, noted that the Court of Appeal had incorrectly reversed the trial decision on the basis of the finding of voluntariness, but that while that error alone was sufficient to dispose of the appeal, it was "important to take this opportunity to set out the proper scope of the confessions rule." The resulting judgment is an unusual synthesis of learned treatise and Supreme Court jurisprudence on a major point of evidentiary law. The following passages are relatively brief excerpts from that judgment:[122]

> As indicated by McLachlin J. (as she then was), in *R. v. Hebert*, [1990] 2 S.C.R. 151, there are two main strands to this Court's jurisprudence under the confessions rule. One approach is narrow, excluding statements only where the police held out explicit threats or promises to the accused. The definitive statement of this approach came in *Ibrahim v. The King*, [1914] A.C. 599 (P.C.), at p. 609:
>
>> It has long been established as a positive rule of English criminal law, that no statement by an accused is admissible in evidence against him unless it is shewn by the prosecution to have been a voluntary statement, in the sense that it has not been obtained from him either by fear of prejudice or hope of advantage exercised or held out by a person in authority.
>
> ...
>
> The *Ibrahim* rule gives the accused only "a negative right — the right not to be tortured or coerced into making a statement by threats or promises held out by a person who is and whom he subjectively believes to be a person in authority": *Hebert, supra*, at p. 165. However, *Hebert* also recognized a second, "much broader" approach, according to which "[t]he absence of violence, threats and promises by the authorities does not necessarily mean that the resulting statement

---

[121] [2000] 2 S.C.R. 3 (S.C.C.).
[122] *Ibid.*, at 22-45.

is voluntary, if the necessary mental element of deciding between alternatives is absent" (p. 166).

While not always followed, McLachlin J. noted at p. 166 that this aspect of the confessions rule "persists as part of our fundamental notion of procedural fairness". This approach is most evident in the so-called "operating mind" doctrine, developed by this Court in *Ward, supra, R. v. Horvath*, [1979] 2 S.C.R. 376, and *R. v. Whittle*, [1994] 2 S.C.R. 914. In those cases the Court made "a further investigation of whether the statements were freely and voluntarily made even if no hope of advantage or fear of prejudice could be found": *Ward, supra*, at p. 40. The "operating mind" doctrine dispelled once and for all the notion that the confessions rule is concerned solely with whether or not the confession was induced by any threats or promises.

These cases focused not just on reliability, but on voluntariness conceived more broadly. None of the reasons in *Ward* or *Horvath* ever expressed any doubts about the reliability of the confessions in issue. Instead, they focused on the lack of voluntariness, whether the cause was shock (*Ward*), hypnosis (*Horvath*, per Beetz J.), or "complete emotional disintegration" (*Horvath, supra*, at p. 400, per Spence J.). Similarly, in *R. v. Hobbins*, [1982] 1 S.C.R. 553, at pp. 556-57, Laskin C.J. noted that in determining the voluntariness of a confession, courts should be alert to the coercive effect of an "atmosphere of oppression", even though there was "no inducement held out of hope of advantage or fear of prejudice, and absent any threats of violence or actual violence"; see also *R. v. Liew*, [1999] 3 S.C.R. 227, at para. 37. Clearly, the confessions rule embraces more than the narrow *Ibrahim* formulation; instead, it is concerned with voluntariness, broadly understood.

2. The *Charter* Era

The *Charter* constitutionalized a new set of protections for accused persons, contained principally in ss. 7 to 14 thereof. The entrenchment of these rights answered certain questions that had once been asked under the aegis of the confessions rule. For example, while the confessions rule did not exclude statements elicited by undercover officers in jail cells (*Rothman, supra*), such confessions can violate the *Charter*: see *Hebert, supra*, and *R. v. Broyles*, [1991] 3 S.C.R. 595.

In *Hebert, supra*, McLachlin J. interpreted the right to silence in light of existing common law protections, such as the confessions rule. However, given the focus of that decision on defining constitutional rights, it did not decide the inverse question: namely, the scope of the common law rules in light of the *Charter*. One possible view is that the *Charter* subsumes the common law rules.

But I do not believe that this view is correct, for several reasons. First, the confessions rule has a broader scope than the *Charter*. For example, the protections of s. 10 only apply "on arrest or detention". By contrast, the confessions rule applies whenever a person in authority questions a suspect. Second, the

Charter applies a different burden and standard of proof from that under the confessions rule. Under the former, the burden is on the accused to show, on a balance of probabilities, a violation of constitutional rights. Under the latter, the burden is on the prosecution to show beyond a reasonable doubt that the confession was voluntary. Finally, the remedies are different. The *Charter* excludes evidence obtained in violation of its provisions under s. 24(2) only if admitting the evidence would bring the administration of justice into disrepute: see *R. v. Stillman*, [1997] 1 S.C.R. 607, *R. v. Collins*, [1987] 1 S.C.R. 265, and the related jurisprudence. By contrast, a violation of the confessions rule always warrants exclusion.

These various differences illustrate that the *Charter* is not an exhaustive catalogue of rights. Instead, it represents a bare minimum below which the law must not fall. A necessary corollary of this statement is that the law, whether by statute or common law, can offer protections beyond those guaranteed by the *Charter*. The common law confessions rule is one such doctrine, and it would be a mistake to confuse it with the protections given by the *Charter*. While obviously it may be appropriate, as in *Hebert, supra*, to interpret one in light of the other, it would be a mistake to assume one subsumes the other entirely.

...

The common law confessions rule is well-suited to protect against false confessions. While its overriding concern is with voluntariness, this concept overlaps with reliability. A confession that is not voluntary will often (though not always) be unreliable. The application of the rule will by necessity be contextual. Hard and fast rules simply cannot account for the variety of circumstances that vitiate the voluntariness of a confession, and would inevitably result in a rule that would be both over- and under-inclusive. A trial judge should therefore consider all the relevant factors when reviewing a confession.

Iacobucci J. goes on to consider such specific impediments to the acceptance of confession evidence as: threats; suggestions of reduced charge or sentence; offers of psychiatric assistance; oppressive detention conditions, such as deprivation of food, clothing, water, sleep, medical attention, access to counsel, or excessively aggressive questioning for a prolonged period of time, or use of non-existent evidence; absence of operating mind; and trickery. The following excerpt from his final summary provides a concise overview:

While the foregoing might suggest that the confessions rule involves a panoply of different considerations and tests, in reality the basic idea is quite simple. First of all, because of the criminal justice system's overriding concern not to convict the innocent, a confession will not be admissible if it is made under circumstances that raise a reasonable doubt as to voluntariness. Both the traditional, narrow *Ibrahim* rule and the oppression doctrine recognize this danger. If the police interrogators subject the suspect to utterly intolerable conditions, or if they offer inducements strong enough to produce an unreliable confession, the trial judge should exclude it. Between these two extremes, oppressive conditions and inducements can operate together to exclude confessions. Trial judges must be alert to the entire circumstances surrounding a confession in making this decision.

Although Iaccobucci says in the preceding quote that the basic idea is "quite simple", facts arising at trials tend to complicate even the simplest of principles. For example, what if the police officer to whom the accused had made a confession was an undercover police officer whom the accused would not have realized was a person in authority; should confession evidence still be excluded in that circumstance? In *R. v. Grandinetti*,[123] Abella J. for the Court said "no". Because the accused had confessed to an undercover officer he thought could influence his murder investigation by enlisting corrupt police officers, the state's coercive power had not been engaged, and the inculpatory statements were therefore not made to a "person in authority".[124]

7. Illegally Obtained Evidence

The common law rule respecting illegally obtained evidence and the change made to it by the *Charter* was summed up by L'Heureux-Dubé J. in *R. v. S. (R.J.)*:[125]

> The most obvious limitation at common law to the principle against self-incrimination was the rule that all relevant evidence, even if obtained illegally, is generally admissible at the trial of an accused. The admission of such evidence appeared to flow from the principle that the criminal law trial is a truth-seeking process and from an emphasis on the reliability of the evidence over all other considerations, including fairness to the accused. This reliability rationale, itself, no doubt partly hinged on an underlying desire for fairness in the criminal process: *R. v. Whittle*, [1994] 2 S.C.R. 914 (per Sopinka J.). This Court's decision in *R. v. Wray*, [1971] S.C.R. 272, permitted a narrow exception to the admission of illegally obtained evidence where admission of the evidence might operate unfairly procedurally, although subsequent decisions were reluctant to adopt unquestioningly this highly limited discretion. The narrow common law rule in *Wray* has now been overruled and the approach is one of weighing probative value against prejudicial effect, with no inquiry into how far probative value exceeds prejudicial effect: *R. v. Potvin*, [1989] 1 S.C.R. 525, at pp. 531-32 (La Forest J. concurring); and *R. v. Seaboyer*, [1991] 2 S.C.R. 577, at pp. 610-11.

---

[123] 2005 SCC 5 (S.C.C.).
[124] *Ibid.*, at para. 44.
[125] [1995] 1 S.C.R. 451 (S.C.C.) at 582-3.

What is more significant for our purposes, however, is that the hue and cry following *Wray* inspired strong legislative action. This action, however, did not take the form of a statutory broadening of the operative principle against self-incrimination. Rather, successive law reform commissions recommended the implementation of statutory provisions that would permit the exclusion of evidence in circumstances in which its admission would bring the administration of justice into disrepute. See Law Reform Commission of Canada, *Report on Evidence* (1975), at p. 22; Ontario Law Reform Commission, *Report on the Law of Evidence* (1976), at p. 94; MacDonald Royal Commission (Second Report), *Freedom and Security under the Law* (1981), vol. 2, at p. 1045; contra: *Report of the Federal/Provincial Task Force on Uniform Rules of Evidence* (1982), at p. 233. Section 24(2) of the *Charter* was therefore very much a procedural relaxation of the near absolute rule of admission of evidence under the common law. It was a remedial rule permitting the exclusion of evidence obtained in violation of one or more substantive rights guaranteed under the *Charter*, where the admission of that evidence would tend to bring the administration of justice into disrepute. Self-incrimination, *per se*, had nothing to do with this change; considerations of fairness and abuse of state power had everything to do with it.

(a) Treatment Under the *Charter*

The introduction of the *Charter* dramatically changed the law regarding the use of improperly obtained evidence, owing to the particular relevance of s. 24, which reads:

24. (1) Anyone whose rights or freedoms, as guaranteed by this *Charter*, have been infringed or denied may apply to a court of competent jurisdiction to obtain such remedy as the court considers appropriate and just in the circumstances.

(2) Where, in proceedings under subsection (1), a court concludes that evidence was obtained in a manner that infringed or denied any rights or freedoms guaranteed by this *Charter*, the evidence shall be excluded if it is established that, having regard to all the circumstances, the admission of it in the proceedings would bring the administration of justice into disrepute.

Initial uncertainty about the application and scope of s. 24 was resolved in *R. v. Collins*.[126] A succinct summary of the law as established by *R. v. Collins* and confirmed in subsequent cases is provided by Lamer C.J. for the majority in *R. v. Caslake*,[127] a case in which the Court dismissed an appeal by a defendant whose impounded car had been searched with neither his permission nor a warrant and found to contain cocaine and a large amount of cash:[128]

---

[126] [1987] 1 S.C.R. 265 (S.C.C.).
[127] [1998] 1 S.C.R. 51 (S.C.C.).
[128] *Ibid.*, at 69-70.

When considering s. 24(2), the test for the exclusion of evidence comes from this Court's decision in *Collins, supra*. There are three categories of factors which must be considered: the fairness of the trial, the seriousness of the *Charter* violation and the possibility that excluding the evidence would bring the administration of justice into greater disrepute than admitting it.

Whether admitting the evidence will have an effect on the fairness of the trial usually depends on whether the evidence was found as a result of conscripting the accused against himself, or whether it was otherwise discoverable. As Cory J. reiterated in *Stillman, supra*, at para. 74, "[t]he admission of evidence which falls into the 'non-conscriptive' category will, as stated in *Collins*, rarely operate to render the trial unfair. If the evidence has been classified as non-conscriptive the court should move on to consider the second and third *Collins* factors...." In this case, the evidence was clearly non-conscriptive. This weighs in favour of admission.

The next category is seriousness of the breach. When considering this issue, the court looks at some or all of the following factors: the obtrusiveness of the search, the individual's expectation of privacy in the area searched, the existence of reasonable and probable grounds; and the good faith of the police....

The third question from *Collins* is whether excluding the evidence would have a more serious impact on the repute of the administration of justice than admitting it. This factor generally relates to the seriousness of the offence and the importance of the evidence to the case for the Crown. In this instance, the prosecution had no case without the evidence. This also weighs in favour of admission.

(b) Civil Litigation

The common law principle that does not provide for exclusion of illegally-obtained evidence in criminal law cases also applies to civil law cases. At best, it may be possible on a preliminary application to obtain an injunction restraining the use of illegally-obtained evidence under the rule in *Lord Ashburton v. Pape*.[129]

In a strongly-worded decision in *Double-E Inc. v. Positive Action Tool Western Ltd.*,[130] however, Muldoon J. indicated his disapproval of the common law inclusionary principle:[131]

> This Court is unwilling to accept the incredibly unjust notion which includes just any means of obtaining evidence, including the illegal, to be a proper jurisprudential basis for overcoming the solicitor-client privilege. For that reason the judicial wilful blindness propounded in *Rolka v. M.N.R.*, [1963] Ex. C.R. 138

---

[129] (1913), [1913] 2 Ch. 469, [1911-13] All E.R. Rep. 708 (Eng. C.A.).

[130] (1988), [1989] 1 F.C. 163 (Fed. T.D.).

[131] *Ibid.*, at 170.

should also be considered out of date. It is a notion which has been repudiated by the *Charter*, even if that constitutional instrument has no specific application in these circumstances. The notion is no longer a fit proposition for Canadian jurisprudence.

It has also been held that to admit into evidence in a family law matter tape recordings made surreptitiously and unlawfully in the family home would bring the administration of justice into disrepute pursuant to s. 24 of the *Charter*.[132]

8. Character

Questions as to the admissibility of evidence of good character are dealt with above, under "self-serving evidence", and are also discussed more specifically below. Evidence of bad character can arise in civil cases, but is obviously most likely to arise in criminal cases. The basic principles in such cases were summed up by Cory J. in *R. v. G. (S.G.)*:[133]

(1) Applicable Principles
It is trite law that "character evidence which shows only that the accused is the type of person likely to have committed the offence in question is inadmissible" (emphasis in original): see for example *Morris v. The Queen*, [1983] 2 S.C.R. 190, at pp. 201-2; *R. v. B. (F.F.)*, [1993] 1 S.C.R. 697, at p. 730. However, there are three general exceptions under which evidence of bad character of the accused can be adduced:

(1) where the evidence is relevant to an issue in the case: see, for example, *Morris, supra*, at p. 202; *B. (F.F.), supra*, at p. 731. See also *R. v. Lepage*, [1995] 1 S.C.R. 654, at pp. 672-74; *R. v. Hinchey*, [1996] 3 S.C.R. 1128, at para. 135, per Cory J.

(2) where the accused puts her character in issue: see, for example, *R. v. McNamara* (No. 1) (1981), 56 C.C.C. (2d) 193 (Ont. C.A.), at p. 352, leave to appeal granted on other grounds (1981), 56 C.C.C. (2d) 576 (S.C.C.);

(3) where the evidence is adduced incidentally to proper cross-examination of the accused on her credibility: see, for example, *Lucas v. The Queen*, [1963] 1 C.C.C. 1 (S.C.C.); *R. v. Chambers*, [1990] 2 S.C.R. 1293.

---

[132] *Seddon v. Seddon* (February 22, 1994), Doc. New Westminster D027618, [1994] B.C.J. No. 1729 (B.C. S.C.).

[133] [1997] 2 S.C.R. 716 (S.C.C.) at 747. Note that although McLachlin J. and L'Heureux-Dubé J. dissented on the ultimate disposition of the appeal, they concurred on the issue of character evidence with Cory J. (Lamer C.J. and Iacobucci J. also concurring).

G. (S.G.) was illustrative of the first of the three exceptions, in that evidence of the accused adult's sexual relationship with one of the juveniles who were her co-accused on murder charges was not adduced simply to show that she was more likely to have committed the crime because of her bad character. Instead, the evidence was relevant to an important issue in the case, namely, the ability of the accused to exercise such exceptional control over the boys that she could persuade them to assault and kill another boy. It was therefore properly admissible, subject to a determination that its probative value outweighed its prejudicial effect. Once the evidence was admitted for that purpose, it could then be used to assess the credibility of her evidence generally:[134]

> The trier of fact will consider all the evidence before it in assessing the general credibility of witnesses, including the accused. A judge sitting alone or a jury has the opportunity to observe demeanour, to hear the testimony of the witnesses and to assess all the evidence presented. All of this will be taken into account in assessing the credibility of the accused, or any other witness. Testimony as to bad character will not be the only evidence that is relevant to credibility. It may be contradicted by the accused's demeanour, or by other evidence supporting the accused. It will simply be one factor among many that will lead the trier of fact to form an impression as to the truthfulness of the accused. Provided an appropriate direction is given, it does not materially increase the risk that the accused will be convicted on the basis of her disposition, rather than for committing the acts that are the subject of the charge.

> As long as evidence of bad character is properly before the jury on an issue in the case, and its prejudicial effect is outweighed by its probative value, then a jury should not be prevented from using the evidence to assess the credibility of the accused.

The nature of the second exception listed above, where evidence of the bad character of an accused is admissible if the accused chooses to give evidence of her good character, is obvious; see below for further discussion of the ambit of this exception. A clear example of the third exception cited — where evidence of bad character is introduced incidental to proper cross-examination of the accused on credibility — is *R. v. Chambers*,[135] cited by Cory J. in the passage from *R. v. G. (S.G.)* above. In *Chambers*, the defence of the accused was that his apparent involvement in a drug smuggling conspiracy was really only an attempt to recapture the affections of his former mistress who was one of the conspirators, despite his admission that he gave every outward appear-

---

[134] *Ibid.*, at 751-2.
[135] [1990] 2 S.C.R. 1293 (S.C.C.).

ance of having entered into the conspiracy. His cross-examination with regard to his drug use, adultery, apparent willingness to bribe political officials and to arrange to have an attorney-general seduced was therefore admissible with regard to credibility, although the jury should properly have been charged that it could not make use of the resulting evidence of his bad character to determine whether he was more likely to have been guilty of entering into the conspiracy.

Note that even if evidence of bad character is admissible pursuant to one of the exceptions noted above, the probative value of the evidence must outweigh its prejudicial effect if it is to be admitted. See, for example, *R. v. B. (F.F.)*:[136]

> Accordingly, evidence which tends to show bad character or a criminal disposition on the part of the accused is admissible if (1) relevant to some other issue beyond disposition or character, and (2) the probative value outweighs the prejudicial effect.

(a) Bad Character of Third Parties

In *R. v. Arcangioli*,[137] the defence of the accused was that he had not stabbed the victim and that this was more likely to have been done by the third party, who had a previous conviction for robbery using a knife. Major J. for the Court noted that:[138]

> However, the danger of a wrongful conviction does not arise where the character evidence pertains not to the accused, but to a third party witness. Consequently, "[s]o long as it is relevant and not otherwise excluded by a rule of evidence, evidence of the bad character of a third party can be adduced by the defence": Sopinka, Lederman and Bryant, supra, at p. 467; *R. v. Scopelliti* (1981), 63 C.C.C. (2d) 481 (Ont. C.A.); and *Wigmore on Evidence* (3rd ed. 1940), vol. 1, sec. 139, at p. 573. The Ontario Court of Appeal confirmed this in *R. v. McMillan* (1975), 23 C.C.C. (2d) 160, aff'd [1977] 2 S.C.R. 824. There, the accused was charged with murdering his child. His defence was that his wife had killed the child. The Court of Appeal held that the accused was permitted to adduce evidence that his wife suffered from a psychopathic personality disorder and had committed acts of violence in the past in order to establish that she had a disposition to commit the offence in question.

> However, evidence of a third party's bad character will not be admitted unless it is relevant. There would be no probative value in evidence that a third party had

---

136 [1993] 1 S.C.R. 697 (S.C.C.) at 731, per Iacobucci J.

137 [1994] 1 S.C.R. 129 (S.C.C.).

138 *Ibid.*, at 139-40.

a propensity to commit the type of act in question if he was otherwise unconnected with the circumstances surrounding the charge, *R. v. McMillan, supra*, at p. 168, per Martin J.A:

> Obviously, unless the third person is connected with the crime under consideration by other circumstances, evidence of such person's disposition to commit the offence is inadmissible on the grounds of lack of probative value. For example, if A is charged with murdering X, in the absence of some nexus with the alleged offence, evidence that B has a propensity or disposition for violence, by itself, is inadmissible to prove B is the murderer because standing alone it has no probative value with respect to the probability of B having committed the offence. If, however, it is proved that A, B and X all lived in the same house when X was killed, and that B had a motive to kill X, then evidence that B had a propensity for violence, may have probative value on the issue whether B, and not A, killed X, and is accordingly admissible.

(b) Evidence of Good Character

It is diverting to imagine the extent to which the trial process would become bogged down if evidence of the good character of all parties and all witnesses were generally admissible, with counsel in effect saying, "The evidence of my witnesses should be given more weight than the evidence of opposing counsel's witnesses, because they are simply better people." Fortunately, evidence of good character is not generally allowed. An overview of the law was provided by the Ontario Court of Appeal in *R. v. Clarke*:[139]

> The general rule of evidence is that a party may not bolster the character of his or her witness until the opposite party has attempted to impeach the witness' character. So-called oath-helping evidence is inadmissible. See *R. v. Béland*, [1987] 2 S.C.R. 298 at 405-408 and *R. v. B. (F.F.),* [1993] 1 S.C.R. 697 at 729-30. There are some exceptions and, for example, within limits the parties are permitted to present their witnesses in the best allowable light. Moreover, the law has always permitted the defence to call character witnesses to testify to the good character of the accused, whether or not the Crown has expressly attempted to impeach the character of the accused. Such evidence is relevant to whether the accused is likely to have committed the offence charged and, if the accused has testified, whether he or she is telling the truth. See: *R. v. Tarrant* (1981), 34 O.R. (2d) 747 (C.A.). Ordinarily, non-expert witnesses may only provide evidence of the good character of the accused by testifying as to the good reputation of the accused in the community. [See Note 1 below] The rules, as I understand them, do not usually permit the witnesses to provide their personal opinion about the accused's character or testify in chief to particular incidents.

---

[139] (1998), [1998] O.J. No. 3521, 1998 CarswellOnt 3447 (Ont. C.A.) at [CarswellOnt] para. 21.

(c) Character Evidence in Civil Trials

There are fewer cases that consider character evidence in civil matters as opposed to criminal matters.[140] In *Deep v. Wood*,[141] Lacourciere J.A. for the Court stated the law as follows:[142]

> Evidence of good character in a civil action is ordinarily inadmissible since it is irrelevant in the determination of most issues arising in those cases. Nevertheless, cross-examination relating to general reputation for untruthfulness or to prior criminal convictions or to findings of professional misconduct involving dishonesty may be used to diminish the credibility of a witness. In contrast, the accused in a criminal case may not be cross-examined as to his character unless he puts it in issue by adducing evidence of good character. See *Criminal Code*, s.593; *R. v. McNamara et al. (No.1)* (1981), 56 C.C.C. (2d) 193 at 342-54. In regard to character evidence in civil matters, Sopinka and Lederman, *op cit.*, pp.288-89, put it as follows:
>
> > There are very few reported cases in which character evidence has been sought to be introduced by the examination of witnesses in chief. The vast majority of cases which deal with the use of character evidence as secondary evidence are cases where such evidence is attempted to be introduced by way of cross-examination. Here character evidence is admitted as part of a broader rule. On cross-examination, subject to the discretion of the trial judge to disallow any question which is vexatious or oppressive, a witness can be asked literally anything as a test of his credibility. This broader rule is subject to the qualification, however, that if the question is irrelevant to the facts in issue, but is asked purely for the purpose of testing credibility, the cross-examiner is bound by the answer. He cannot lead evidence to contradict the witness.
> >
> > In turn the rule precluding rebuttal evidence is subject to a number of exceptions.
>
> Among the recognized exceptions under which a cross-examiner may introduce contradictory evidence is the proof that a witness has previously been convicted of a criminal offence. At p.291 the learned authors comment:
>
> > This is a statutory exception to the rule that answers on collateral matters are conclusive. It has been held in Ontario that the use of the word "crime" in the *Ontario Evidence Act* restricts such questions to offences created by Federal legislation. While this exception allows a specific act tending to show bad character to be introduced, it is a tactic that is seldom used and is unpopular with trial judges in civil cases.

---

[140] A fact that was noted by Finch J.A. in *Tsoukas v. Segura*, 2001 BCCA 664 (B.C. C.A.) at para. 47.

[141] (1983), 143 D.L.R. (3d) 246 (Ont. C.A.) at 250.

[142] *Ibid.*, at 250.

Sopinka was also quoted with approval in *Conesa v. Bekessy*,[143] in which the British Columbia Court of Appeal upheld a trial judge's reliance upon its statement that while a witness can be asked anything as a test of credibility, if the question is irrelevant to the facts in issue, the examiner is bound by the answer given and cannot lead evidence to contradict the witness.

9. Criminal Record

As discussed in the preceding section on character, evidence of the bad character of an accused is generally admissible only if the accused has put character in evidence, while evidence of the bad character of a third party witness is more generally admissible. While evidence of prior criminal convictions is evidence of bad character, there are specific rules, including specific statutory provisions, which also have a bearing on evidence of a criminal record.

Relevant *Criminal Code* provisions include s. 666:

> 666. Where, at a trial, the accused adduces evidence of his good character, the prosecutor may, in answer thereto, before a verdict is returned, adduce evidence of the previous conviction of the accused for any offences, including any previous conviction by reason of which a greater punishment may be imposed.

Section 12(1) and (1.1) of the *Canada Evidence Act* are as follows:

> 12. (1) A witness may be questioned as to whether the witness has been convicted of any offence, excluding any offence designated as a contravention under the *Contraventions Act*, but including such an offence where the conviction was entered after a trial on an indictment.
>
> (1.1) If the witness either denies the fact or refuses to answer, the opposite party may prove the conviction.

In *R. v. Corbett*,[144] a case in which the constitutionality of s. 12 of the *Canada Evidence Act* was upheld, Dickson C.J. noted the policy rationale for allowing evidence of prior convictions:[145]

> Cross-examination of an accused with respect to prior convictions has been permitted in Canada since an accused first became competent to testify on his

---

[143] (1988), 1988 CarswellBC 1446, [1989] B.C.W.L.D. 257, [1989] C.L.D. 201 (B.C. C.A.).

[144] [1988] 1 S.C.R. 670 (S.C.C.).

[145] *Ibid.*, at 685-6.

own behalf in 1893: *R. v. D'Aoust* (1902), 5 C.C.C. 407 (Ont. C.A.). What lies behind s. 12 is a legislative judgment that prior convictions do bear upon the credibility of a witness. In deciding whether or not to believe someone who takes the stand, the jury will quite naturally take a variety of factors into account. They will observe the demeanour of the witness as he or she testifies, the witness' appearance, tone of voice, and general manner. Similarly, the jury will take into account any information it has relating to the witness' habits or mode of life. There can surely be little argument that a prior criminal record is a fact which, to some extent at least, bears upon the credibility of a witness. Of course, the mere fact that a witness was previously convicted of an offence does not mean that he or she necessarily should not be believed, but it is a fact which a jury might take into account in assessing credibility.

This rationale for s. 12 has been explicit in the case law. See, e.g., *R. v. Stratton*, *supra*, at p. 461, per Martin J.A., "Unquestionably, the theory upon which prior convictions are admitted in relation to credibility is that the character of the witness, as evidenced by the prior conviction or convictions, is a relevant fact in assessing the testimonial reliability of the witness."

Similarly, in *R. v. Brown* (1978), 38 C.C.C. (2d) 339 (Ont. C.A.), at p. 342, per Martin J.A., "The fact that a witness has been convicted of a crime is relevant to his trustworthiness as a witness."

An American court identified the rationale behind a similar rule in the following language:

> What a person is often determines whether he should be believed. When a defendant voluntarily testifies in a criminal case, he asks the jury to accept his word. No sufficient reason appears why the jury should not be informed what sort of person is asking them to take his word. In transactions of everyday life this is probably the first thing that they would wish to know. So it seems to us in a real sense that when a defendant goes onto a stand, "he takes his character with him...." Lack of trustworthiness may be evinced by his abiding and repeated contempt for laws which he is legally and morally bound to obey, as in the case at bar, though the violations are not concerned solely with crimes involving "dishonesty and false statement."

Corbett was also notable for settling the question of whether or not a trial judge has the discretion to disallow evidence of prior convictions if the probative value is outweighed by the prejudicial value. Although La Forest J. dissented on the ultimate outcome of the case, Dickson C.J. for the majority agreed with him on the point that a trial judge does have the discretion to disallow evidence of prior convictions:[146]

---

[146] *Ibid.*, at 697. It is, however, the "usual course" that an accused who chooses to testify will be cross-examined on their criminal record: *R. v. P. (N.A.)* (2002), [2002] O.J. No. 4829, 2002 CarswellOnt 4284 (Ont. C.A.) at para. 20, per Doherty J.A.

I agree with my colleague, La Forest J., that basic principles of the law of evidence embody an inclusionary policy which would permit into evidence everything logically probative of some fact in issue, subject to the recognized rules of exclusion and exceptions thereto. Thereafter the question is one of weight. The evidence may carry much weight, little weight, or no weight at all. If error is to be made it should be on the side of inclusion rather than exclusion and our efforts in my opinion, consistent with the ever-increasing openness of our society, should be toward admissibility unless a very clear ground of policy or law dictates exclusion.

I agree with La Forest J. that the trial judge has a discretion to exclude prejudicial evidence of previous convictions in an appropriate case.

With regard to the factors that might be relevant in exercising that discretion, La Forest J. stated:[147]

It is impossible to provide an exhaustive catalogue of the factors that are relevant in assessing the probative value or potential prejudice of such evidence, but among the most important are the nature of the previous conviction and its remoteness or nearness to the present charge.

Among the specific factors mentioned in this regard were whether the previous conviction was for acts such as deceit or fraud that reflect directly on integrity, the similarity of the previous conviction to the charge faced by the accused, the temporal remoteness of the previous offence, and the unfairness of shielding the accused if the prosecution's witnesses have been attacked on credibility.

The decision in *Corbett* gave rise to the question of when an application to exclude evidence of prior convictions should be made. This was answered in *R. v. Underwood*,[148] per Lamer C.J. for the Court:[149]

In summary, a *Corbett* application should be made after the close of the Crown's case. If the trial judge believes it to be necessary, a *voir dire* should be held in which the defence discloses what evidence it intends to call, so he or she can make a fully informed ruling on the application. This ruling may be subject to modification if the defence evidence departs significantly from what was disclosed.

The ruling on the *Corbett* application may be crucial in defence counsel's strategic decision on adducing the testimony of the accused.

---

[147] *Ibid.*, at 740.
[148] [1998] 1 S.C.R. 77 (S.C.C.).
[149] *Ibid.*, at 83-4.

10. Similar Fact

The preceding sections on character evidence and criminal records discussed the general rules that establish that evidence of past misdeeds may be inadmissible. Even though similar fact evidence is presumptively inadmissible, there will still be cases where evidence of similar facts is admissible under the "similar fact rule".

(a) Overview

The history and parameters of this rule were most thoroughly canvassed by McLachlin J. for the majority in *R. v. B. (C.R.)*.[150] In the following passage from *B. (C.R.)*, she summarized and quoted from the seminal case, *Makin v. Attorney General for New South Wales*:[151]

> Viewed thus, the so-called similar fact rule was in reality an exception — narrowly defined — to the general rule excluding evidence of prior misconduct or propensity.
>
> This approach is embodied in the oft-quoted passage from *Makin v. Attorney General for New South Wales*, [1894] A.C. 57, at p. 65. Lord Herschell L.C. first enunciated the general principle of exclusion (the first limb of the rule):
>
>> It is undoubtedly not competent for the prosecution to adduce evidence tending to shew that the accused has been guilty of criminal acts other than those covered by the indictment, for the purpose of leading to the conclusion that the accused is a person likely from his criminal conduct or character to have committed the offence for which he is being tried.
>
> He then stated the exception (the second limb of the rule), at p. 65:
>
>> On the other hand, the mere fact that the evidence adduced tends to shew the commission of other crimes does not render it inadmissible if it be relevant to an issue before the jury, and it may be so relevant if it bears upon the question whether the acts alleged to constitute the crime charged in the indictment were designed or accidental, or to rebut a defence which would otherwise be open to the accused.
>
> From the point of view of underlying principle, the *Makin* rule may be seen as essentially concerned with probative value. On the one hand, it recognized the

---

[150] [1990] 1 S.C.R. 717 (S.C.C.). Subsequently, the decision in *B. (C.R.)* has been repeatedly recognized by the Supreme Court of Canada as the governing authority. See *R. v. Handy*, [2002] 2 S.C.R. 908 (S.C.C.) at para. 53.

[151] *Ibid.* at 724-6.

grave prejudice that evidence of previous wrongdoing or propensity might work. Such evidence often does not possess great logical or probative force. Yet at the same time it has great potential for harm, raising the danger that the jury may convict, not because they are satisfied that the Crown has proved beyond a reasonable doubt that the accused committed the offence with which he stands charged, but because the accused is a bad or suspicious person. On the other hand, the *Makin* rule acknowledged the common sense proposition that in some cases the probative value of the evidence might justify its reception.

As a rule of application the analysis in *Makin* typically involved two steps. Courts first asked whether the proposed evidence went beyond mere propensity. If that hurdle was met, they went on to determine whether the evidence fell within one of the accepted exclusionary categories. In practice, the two steps often merged since evidence falling within the established categories of exception to the general exclusionary rule usually went beyond mere propensity.

After an extensive review of the jurisprudence, McLachlin J. then drew the following conclusions:[152]

This review of the jurisprudence leads me to the following conclusions as to the law of similar fact evidence as it now stands in Canada. The analysis of whether the evidence in question is admissible must begin with the recognition of the general exclusionary rule against evidence going merely to disposition. As affirmed in *Boardman* and reiterated by this Court in *Guay*, *Cloutier*, *Morris*, *Morin* and *D. (L.E.)*, evidence which is adduced solely to show that the accused is the sort of person likely to have committed an offence is, as a rule, inadmissible. Whether the evidence in question constitutes an exception to this general rule depends on whether the probative value of the proposed evidence outweighs its prejudicial effect. In a case such as the present, where the similar fact evidence sought to be adduced is prosecution evidence of a morally repugnant act committed by the accused, the potential prejudice is great and the probative value of the evidence must be high indeed to permit its reception. The judge must consider such factors as the degree of distinctiveness or uniqueness between the similar fact evidence and the offences alleged against the accused, as well as the connection, if any, of the evidence to issues other than propensity, to the end of determining whether, in the context of the case before him, the probative value of the evidence outweighs its potential prejudice and justifies its reception.

It should be noted that the contemporary principled approach elucidated in *B. (C.R.)* and other recent cases is a departure from the approach taken in some older cases, and that the latter should be viewed with reservation. As noted by McIntyre J. in *R. v. Sweitzer*:[153]

---

[152] *Ibid.*, at 734-5.
[153] [1982] 1 S.C.R. 949 (S.C.C.) at 952-3.

Over the years in seeking to apply this principle judges have tended to create a list of categories or types of cases in which similar fact evidence could be admitted, generally by reference to the purpose for which the evidence was adduced. Evidence of similar facts has been adduced to prove intent, to prove a system, to prove a plan, to show malice, to rebut the defence of accident or mistake, to prove identity, to rebut the defence of innocent association, and for other similar and related purposes. This list is not complete.

This approach has been useful because similar fact evidence by its nature is frequently adduced for its relevance to a single issue in the case under trial. It has however involved, in my opinion, a tendency to overlook the true basis upon which evidence of similar facts is admissible. The general principle described by Lord Herschell may and should be applied in all cases where similar fact evidence is tendered and its admissibility will depend upon the probative effect of the evidence balanced against the prejudice caused to the accused by its admission whatever the purpose of its admission.

Given that the rule in question is termed the "similar fact rule", the question might arise of how similar the facts must be for it to apply. In *R. v. C. (M.H.)*,[154] McLachlin J. stated:[155]

There will be occasions, however, where the similar act evidence will go to more than disposition, and will be considered to have real probative value. That probative value usually arises from the fact that the acts compared are so unusual and strikingly similar that their similarities cannot be attributed to coincidence. Only where the probative force clearly outweighs the prejudice, or the danger that the jury may convict for non-logical reasons, should such evidence be received.

The Court retreated from the use of the term "strikingly similar", however, as noted in *R. v. Arp*,[156] per Cory J. for the Court:[157]

The probative value must, of course, significantly outweigh the prejudice to the accused for the evidence to be admissible. See *B. (C.R.)*, supra. However, the majority in *B. (C.R.)*, at pp. 732-33, rejected the proposition that the evidence must show a "striking similarity" between the acts in question in order for the evidence to have the requisite probative value. I agree that the requirement of "striking similarity" needs to be qualified.

The approach taken by Cory J. in *Arp* refers instead to how unlikely it is that similar facts are the result of coincidence:[158]

---

[154] [1991] 1 S.C.R. 763 (S.C.C.).
[155] *Ibid.*, at 771-2.
[156] [1998] 3 S.C.R. 339 (S.C.C.).
[157] *Ibid.*, at 364.
[158] *Ibid.*, at 365-6.

Instead, a principled approach to the admission of similar fact evidence will in all cases rest on the finding that the accused's involvement in the alleged similar acts or counts is unlikely to be the product of coincidence. This conclusion ensures that the evidence has sufficient probative force to be admitted, and will involve different considerations in different contexts. Where, as here, similar fact evidence is adduced on the issue of identity, there must be a high degree of similarity between the acts for the evidence to be admitted. For example, a unique trademark or signature will automatically render the alleged acts "strikingly similar" and therefore highly probative and admissible. In the same way, a number of significant similarities, taken together, may be such that by their cumulative effect, they warrant admission of the evidence.

(b) Propensity

In reading the preceding section on similar fact evidence, the reader may be left with the impression that the courts will allow evidence of facts that are so similar as to be distinctive — the trademark glove left by the "Phantom" at the scenes of his burglaries in the "Pink Panther" films comes to mind — but that the courts will still refuse to allow evidence that just goes to show the mere propensity of an accused to commit crimes. A closer reading, however, will show that contemporary courts are indeed willing to admit evidence to show the propensity of an accused to commit a crime in some circumstances. They would certainly balk at evidence that merely showed that an accused was a bad person in a generic sense, but would now seem willing to acknowledge that evidence that shows that an accused has established a pattern of being bad in a particular way may be admissible.

In *R. v. Handy*,[159] Binnie J. considered whether evidence of the ex-wife of the accused as to his propensity for violent, hurtful sex should have been admitted in his trial for sexual assault of an acquaintance. Although a retrial was ordered, this was principally because the trial judge had failed to deal with allegations of collusion between the ex-wife and the complainant before referring the case to the jury. On the question of whether evidence of propensity should be admissible, however, Binnie J. took some pains to show, by referring to isolated quotations from numerous cases, that it was. His statement of a general principle regarding propensity was that:[160]

> Canadian case law recognizes that as the "similar facts" become more focussed and specific to circumstances similar to the charge (i.e., more situation specific),

---

[159] [2002] 2 S.C.R. 908 (S.C.C.).
[160] *Ibid.,* at para. 48.

the probable value of propensity, thus circumscribed, becomes more cogent. As the differences and variables that distinguish the earlier "similar facts" from the subject matter of the charge in this type of case are reduced, the cogency of the desired inferences is thought to increase. Ultimately the policy premise of the general exclusionary rule (prejudice exceeds probative value) ceases to be true.

(c) Similar Fact Evidence In Civil Cases

As is noted elsewhere in this volume, the general rule is that the law of evidence is the same for civil and for criminal law. That this is specifically the case with regard to similar fact evidence has been noted by the Ontario Court of Appeal in *Greenglass v. Rusonik*:[161]

> The principles governing similar fact evidence have equal application to both civil and criminal proceedings: see *Phipson on Evidence* (12th ed.) para. 491, pp. 441-442; and *Wigmore on Evidence* (2d ed.) vol. 2, para. 371. Lord Denning stated in *Mood Music Publishing Co. Ltd. v. De Wolfe Ltd.*, [1976] 1 All E.R. 736 at 766:

> The admissibility of evidence as to 'similar facts' has been much considered in the criminal law....The criminal courts have been very careful not to admit such evidence unless its probative value is so strong that it should be received in the interests of justice: and its admission will not operate unfairly to the accused. In civil cases the courts have followed a similar line but have not been so chary of admitting it. In civil cases the courts will admit evidence of similar facts if it is logically probative, that is, if it is logically relevant in determining the matter which is in issue: provided that it is not oppressive or unfair to the other side: and also that the other side has fair notice of it and is able to deal with it.

The British Columbia Court of Appeal in *Statton v. Johnson*[162] also found that the similar fact rule operates virtually identically in civil and criminal cases:[163]

> I doubt that there is any difference between admissibility of evidence in civil and criminal cases, with the possible exception that in the latter class of case, particularly cases tried before a jury, there may be a heightened concern that potentially prejudicial evidence not be placed before the trier of fact unless it has significant probative value.

It might be thought that, on principle, the seriousness of the consequences facing the unsuccessful party in a civil case would have some

---

[161] (March 18, 1983), Arnup, Blair, Weatherston JJ.A., [1983] O.J. No. 40 (Ont. C.A.) at para. 42.
[162] (1999), [1999] B.C.J. No 621, 1999 CarswellBC 545 (B.C. C.A.).
[163] *Ibid.*, at [CarswellBC] para. 45.

bearing on a court's willingness or reluctance to admit similar fact evidence. The case law, however, would not seem to support such an approach.

11. Public Interest Immunity

Certain types of evidence which might otherwise be adduced can be exempted from disclosure if their production might harm the public interest. Examples include the identity of police informers and matters affecting national security.

(a) The Competing Values

The fundamental tension between two competing public interests was noted by La Forest J. for the Court in *Carey v. Ontario*:[164]

> It is obviously necessary for the proper administration of justice that litigants have access to all evidence that may be of assistance to the fair disposition of the issues arising in litigation. It is equally clear, however, that certain information regarding governmental activities should not be disclosed in the public interest.

If the public interest in non-disclosure outweighs the judicial interest in disclosure, then the information is not disclosed.

(b) An "Immunity" Rather Than a "Privilege"

The exact legal nature of the right to withhold documents and the question of who can trigger that right is sometimes contentious. This is clarified in *Carey v. Ontario*:[165]

> The public interest in the non-disclosure of a document is not, as Thorson J.A. noted in the Court of Appeal, a Crown Privilege. Rather, it is more properly called a public interest immunity, one that, in the final analysis, is for the court to weigh. The court may itself raise the issue of its application, as indeed counsel may, but the most usual and appropriate way to raise it is by means of a certificate by the affidavit of a Minister or where, as in this case, a statute permits it or it is otherwise appropriate, of a senior public servant.

---

[164] [1986] 2 S.C.R. 637 (S.C.C.) at 647.
[165] *Ibid.*, at 653.

(c) The Courts as Final Arbiter

It has sometimes been asserted that an assertion by government of the immunity is final and conclusive, a view that the Supreme Court of Canada did not accept:[166]

> The House [House of Lords in *Conway v. Rimmer*, [1968] A.C. 910] firmly rejected the notion that the Minister's statement was final and conclusive. It was the courts that must determine the balance to be struck between the public interest in the proper administration of justice and the public interest in withholding certain documents or other evidence. Proper deference should, of course, be given to the Minister's views, particularly in relation to objections to production of particular documents on the basis of their contents, or where the Minister's reasons involve considerations that cannot properly be weighed on the basis of judicial experience....In assessing whether documents should be produced or not, the court could in some cases come to a decision one way or the other on the basis of the Minister's statement alone, but in case of doubt the judge could inspect them.

(d) Claims Based Upon Avoiding Disclosure of Police Informant Identity

Assertions of public interest immunity in order to protect the identity of police informers are accorded significant deference by the courts:[167]

> Where the public interest claim is based on an assertion of police informant privilege, the claim will, if substantiated, of necessity succeed at the preliminary inquiry stage. The police informant privilege must prevail unless disclosure is required to demonstrate the innocence of the accused: *R. v. Leipert* (1997), 112 C.C.C. (3d) 385 at p. 394-95, 41 C.R.R. (2d) 266 (S.C.C.).

(e) Relationship Between Common Law and Statute

The *Canada Evidence Act*, R.S.C. 1985, c. C-5, ss. 37-39, sets out procedures by which the courts may determine objections to the disclosure of evidence on public interest grounds, specifically including grounds of injury to international relations or security (s. 38) and confidence of the Queen's Privy Council (s. 39). In considering the nature

---

[166] *Ibid.*
[167] *R. v. Richards* (1997), 34 O.R. (3d) 244 (Ont. C.A.) at 248.

of the statutory provisions, the Ontario Court of Appeal stated in *R. v. Richards*:[168]

> Section 37 does not create or define the public interest privilege. That privilege is a creature of the common law rules of evidence. Section 37 provides a mechanism for the resolution of a privilege claim."

The mechanism that s. 37 provides for resolution of a privilege claim is not entirely satisfactory. It appears, for example, that immunity claims can be made before bodies other than superior courts, such as administrative tribunals.[169] Where this occurs, however, it is not clear whether the onus to make an application to determine the immunity pursuant to s. 37(3) and (4) is on the party that has asserted it or on the party that sought to adduce the evidence.

12. Best Evidence Rule

The best evidence rule is greatly reduced in importance in the technology-driven, contemporary world of faxes, photocopies, e-mails and electronic recordings, particularly in light of statutory provisions such as s. 24 of the *Canada Evidence Act* that specifically allow their introduction as evidence. Many would agree with the judge[170] who noted that:

> As the use of copies, counsel, Mr. Wood, the best evidence rule is a dodo. It's gone in the way of the dodo bird.

For most purposes, then, counsel are safe to either ignore the best evidence rule altogether, or to rely on a simplified statement of the modern interpretation of the rule, such as that of the B.C. Court of Appeal in *Shaghaghi v. Mozaffarian*:[171]

> The "best evidence" rule is not enforced with the strictness that it once was. This Court considered the modern application of the rule in R. v. Betterest Vinyl Manufacturing Ltd. et al. (1989), 52 C.C.C. (3d) 441 and concluded that it is now limited to requiring a party to produce the original if it is available. Secondary evidence of the contents of a document may be admitted when the failure to produce the original is explained.

---

[168] *Ibid.*, at 247.

[169] *See Babcock v. Canada (Attorney General)*, 2002 SCC 57 (S.C.C.) at paras. 42-4, where McLachlin C.J. in *obiter* expresses the view that there is no impediment to this practice.

[170] Kennedy A.C.J., quoted in *R. v. Wood* (2001), 2001 CarswellNS 72 (N.S. C.A.) at para. 80.

[171] 2002 BCCA 531 (B.C. C.A.) at para. 22.

Since the rule does still occasionally arise in argument, however, such as when the requirements of the *Canada Evidence Act* for the admission of photocopies have not been complied with,[172] it may still be necessary for counsel to have an understanding of the rule. The following passage from the judgment of Pigeon J. in *R. v. Cotroni*[173] provides a useful resource in this regard. The issue in that case was whether re-recordings should be admitted where original tape recordings had been innocently destroyed:[174]

Of the "best evidence" rule Halsbury states in the 4th ed., Vol. 17, p. 8:

"That evidence should be the best that the nature of the case will allow is, besides being a matter of obvious prudence, a principle with a considerable pedigree. However, any strict interpretation of this principle has long been obsolete, and the rule is now only of importance in regard to the primary evidence of private documents. The logic of requiring the production of an original document where it is available rather than relying on possibly un-satisfactory copies, or the recollections of witnesses, is clear, although modern techniques make objections to the first alternative less strong."

The rule itself, in its relatively modern form did not absolutely exclude secondary evidence. It is stated by Lord Esher, M.R. in *Lucas v. Williams & Sons*, (1892) 2 Q.B. 113 at 116:

"'Primary' and 'secondary' evidence mean this: primary evidence is evidence which the law requires to be given first; secondary evidence is evidence which may be given in the absence of the better evidence which the law requires to be given first, when a proper explanation is given of the absence of that better evidence."

Lord Denning would remove the question of secondary evidence entirely from the area of admissibility to that of weight. In *Garton v. Hunter*, (1969) 2 Q.B. 37 at 44 he said:

"It is plain that Scott, L.J. had in mind the old rule that a party must produce the best evidence that the nature of the case will allow, and that any less good evidence is to be excluded. That old rule has gone by the board long ago. The only remaining instance of it that I know is that if an original document is available in your hands, you must produce it. You cannot give secondary evidence by producing a copy. Nowadays we do not confine ourselves to the best evidence. We admit all relevant evidence. The goodness or badness of it goes only to weight, and not to admissibility."

---

[172] See, for example, *R. v. S. (H.M.L.)*, 2005 BCPC 337 (B.C. Prov. Ct.).

[173] *(sub nom. Papalia v. R.)* [1979] 2 S.C.R. 256.

[174] *Ibid.*, at 263-4.

However, the counsel of prudence mentioned by Halsbury accords with the principle stated by *McCormick on Evidence*, 2nd ed. at p. 571:

> If the original document has been destroyed by the person who offers evidence of its contents, the evidence is not admissible unless, by showing that the destruction was accidental or was done in good faith, without intention to prevent its use as evidence, he rebuts to the satisfaction of the trial judge, any inference of fraud.

That the rule does retain some importance today can be understood by considering, for example, how much value counsel can make of marginalia, erasures and other aspects of original documents that can be lost in photocopied documents.

13. Prejudicial

Much of the discussion in preceding sections has involved questions of whether the probative value of evidence outweighs its prejudicial effect in the context of specific evidentiary rules. Highly inflammatory evidence, such as photographs, or evidence of past criminal convictions or bad character, for example, may be objected to as being prejudicial.

What does "prejudicial" mean with regard to evidence? In *R. v. MacDonald*,[175] the Ontario Court of Appeal quoted from *McCormick on Evidence*:[176]

> Consequently, demonstrative evidence is frequently objected to as **prejudicial**, a term which is today generally **defined as** suggesting "decision on an improper basis, commonly, though not necessarily, an emotional one."

In *R. v. B. (L.)*,[177] Charron J.A. for the Court provided a list which was "not meant to be exhaustive" of factors to consider in evaluating prejudice:[178]

> In assessing the prejudicial effect of the proposed evidence, consideration should be given to such matters as:
> (i)   how discreditable it is;
> (ii) the extent to which it may support an inference of guilt based solely on bad character;
> (iii) the extent to which it may confuse issues; and

---

[175] (2000), 49 O.R. (3d) 417 (Ont. C.A.).
[176] *Ibid.*, at 428.
[177] (1997), (sub nom. *R. v. G. (M.A.)*) 116 C.C.C. (3d) 481 (Ont. C.A.).
[178] *Ibid.*, at 494.

(iv) the accused's ability to respond to it.

Note that although *Phipson On Evidence* has categorized prejudice into disposition prejudice, reasoning prejudice, bad person prejudice, accumulation prejudice and diversion prejudice,[179] it would appear that no Canadian court has adopted that categorization.

14. The Rule in *Browne v. Dunn* (Failure to Cross-Examine)

The "rule in *Browne v. Dunn*"[180] — namely that counsel who have not cross-examined a witness on a point can neither impeach the witness on extrinsic evidence nor argue that the witness should be disbelieved — has been sufficiently controversial in Canada to have prompted one judge to ask, "Is there a rule in *Browne v. Dunn*?"[181] That question was recently answered in the affirmative by the Supreme Court of Canada.[182] The rule is not, however, an inflexible one.

The following are the passages cited from *Browne v. Dunn* that give rise to the rule. Lord Herschell L.C. stated:[183]

> Now, my Lords, I cannot help saying that it seems to me to be absolutely essential to the proper conduct of a cause, where it is intended to suggest that a witness is not speaking the truth on a particular point, to direct his attention to the fact by some questions put in cross-examination showing that that imputation is intended to be made, and not to take his evidence and pass it by as a matter altogether unchallenged, and then, when it is impossible for him to explain, as perhaps he might have been able to do if such questions had been put to him, the circumstances which it is suggested indicate that the story he tells ought not to be believed, to argue that he is a witness unworthy of credit. My Lords. I have always understood that if you intend to impeach a witness you are bound, whilst he is in the box, to give him an opportunity of making any explanation which is open to him; and, as it seems to me, that is not only a rule of professional practice in the conduct of a case, but is essential to fair play and fair dealing with witnesses. Sometimes reflections have been made upon excessive cross-examination of witnesses, and it has been complained of as undue; but it seems to me that a cross-examination of a witness which errs in the direction of excess may be far more fair to him than to leave him without cross-examination, and afterwards to suggest that he is not a witness of truth, I mean upon a point on which it is not otherwise

---

[179] *Phipson On Evidence*, 15th edition (London: Sweet & Maxwell, 2000), pp. 390-2.

[180] (1893), 6 R. 67 (U.K. H.L.).

[181] Macdonald J. in *Stewart v. Canadian Broadcasting Corp.* (1997), 150 D.L.R. (4th) 24 (Ont. Gen. Div.) at 175, additional reasons at (1997), 152 D.L.R. (4th) 102 (Ont. Gen. Div.).

[182] *R. v. Lyttle*, 2004 SCC 5 (S.C.C.) at paras. 64-5.

[183] *Supra*, note 180 at 70-1.

perfectly clear that he has had full notice beforehand that there is an intention to impeach the credibility of the story which he is telling. Of course I do not deny for a moment that there are cases in which that notice has been so distinctly and unmistakably given, and the point upon which he is impeached, and is to be impeached, is so manifest, that it is not necessary to waste time in putting questions to him upon it. All I am saying is that it will not do to impeach the credibility of a witness upon a matter on which he has not had any opportunity of giving an explanation by reason of there having been no suggestion whatever in the course of the case that his story is not accepted.

Lord Halsbury stated:[184]

My Lords, with regard to the manner in which the evidence was given in this case, I cannot too heartily express my concurrence with the Lord Chancellor as to the mode in which a trial should be conducted. To my mind nothing would be more absolutely unjust than not to cross-examine witnesses upon evidence which they have given, so as to give them notice, and to give them an opportunity of explanation, and an opportunity very often to defend their own character, and, not having given them such an opportunity, to ask the jury afterwards to disbelieve what they have said, although not one question has been directed either to their credit or to the accuracy of the facts they have deposed to.

And Lord Morris stated:[185]

My Lords, there is another point upon which I would wish to guard myself, namely, with respect to laying down any hard-and-fast rule as regards cross-examining a witness as a necessary preliminary to impeaching his credit. In this case, I am clearly of opinion that the witnesses, having given their testimony, and not having been cross-examined, having deposed to a state of facts which is quite reconcilable with the rest of the case, and which the fact of the retainer having been given, it was impossible for the plaintiff to ask the jury at the trial, and is impossible for him to ask any legal tribunal, to say that those witnesses are not to be credited. But I can quite understand the case in which a story told by a witness may have been of so incredible and romancing a character that the most effective cross-examination would be to ask him to leave the box. I therefore wish it to be understood that I would not concur in ruling that it was necessary, in order to impeach a witness's credit, that you should take him through the story which he had told, giving him notice by the questions that you impeached his credit.

The Supreme Court of Canada did rely on *Browne v. Dunn* in *Peters v. Perras*,[186] but until recently had had little subsequent opportunity to consider it. In *R. v. Palmer,*[187] McIntyre J. for the Court had

---

[184] *Ibid.*, at 76-7.
[185] *Ibid.*, at 79.
[186] (1909), 42 S.C.R. 244 (S.C.C.).
[187] (1979), [1980] 1 S.C.R. 759 (S.C.C.).

indicated his agreement with the more flexible version of the rule enunciated in the judgment of Lord Morris.[188] Most recently, in *R. v. Lyttle*,[189] the Court has once again endorsed a flexible version of the rule, quoting the preceding passage from Lord Herschell, but then adding:[190]

> The rule, although designed to provide fairness to witnesses and the parties, is not fixed. The extent of its application is within the discretion of the trial judge after taking into account all the circumstances of the case. See *R. v. Palmer* (1979), [1980] 1 S.C.R. 759 (S.C.C.), at pp. 781-82; J. Sopinka, S.N. Lederman and A.W. Bryant, *The Law of Evidence in Canada* (2nd ed. 1999), at pp. 954-57. In any event, the foregoing rule in *Browne v. Dunn* remains a sound principle of general application, though irrelevant to the issue before the trial judge in this case.

---

[188] *Ibid.*, at 781-2.
[189] 2004 SCC 5.
[190] *Ibid.*, at para. 65.

6

IS THERE A PROBLEM WITH THE FORM OF THE QUESTION?

As noted in the introduction, the purpose of this book is to serve as a courtroom reference in support of evidentiary arguments. Many of the objections which give rise to such arguments are on topics covered in the preceding sections, topics which are commonly found in evidence texts. At other times, however, arguments are prompted by questions that are not objectionable because the evidence that would be produced by a responsive answer must necessarily violate one of the rules of evidence, but because the question itself is objectionable. As the Supreme Court of Canada noted in *R. v. Lyttle,*[1] for example:[2]

> Counsel are bound by the rules of relevancy and barred from resorting to harassment, misrepresentation, repetitiousness or, more generally, from putting questions whose prejudicial effect outweighs their probative value.

Most of these grounds of objection are so well-known that Canadian courts have not had to confirm their existence in any reported decision. Of those decisions that are cited below, some are from cases that considered questions that were asked on discovery rather than at trial; given that latitude for questions upon discovery is generally greater than for questions at trial, evidentiary problems at discovery will normally be equally problematic at trial.

1. Ambiguous or Vague

Ambiguous or vague questions are objectionable.[3]

---

[1] 2004 SCC 5 (S.C.C.).

[2] *Ibid.*, at para. 44.

[3] *Ortega v. 1005640 Ontario Inc.* (1999), [1999] O.J. No. 2432, 1999 CarswellOnt 2002 (Ont. Master). In *Parkridge Homes Ltd. v. Anglin* (1996), [1996] A.J. No. 768, 1996 CarswellAlta 1136 (Alta. Q.B.) at para. 40, Rooke J. accepted submissions that vague or ambiguous questions were improper or inadmissible on cross-examination.

2. Argumentative

The Ontario Court of Appeal in *R. v. Buxbaum*[4] expressed the following view on the distinction between questions that are objectionable as argumentative and those that are not:[5]

> We agree with Mr. Ruby's submission that a question is not improper as argumentative when its purpose is to obtain an answer, even though the question is put in the suggestive form and requires the witness to agree or disagree. Although an answer to such a question will have little weight in some circumstances, the question is not necessarily impermissible as being argumentative. An argumentative question is one that invokes the witness' assent to the questioner's inferences or, in other words, is one which assumes as true matters to which the witness has not testified and which are in dispute between the parties.

A trial judge is entitled to intervene to cut off argumentative questions.[6]

3. Assuming Facts Not in Evidence

Although it may be objectionable for a question to assume a fact not in evidence, the Nova Scotia Court of Appeal in *R. v. Wood*[7] did not accept the argument that such questions were improper where the trial judge had carefully directed the jury that it would be for them to determine, on the basis of admissible evidence, whether any of the underlying transactions had actually taken place and that the Crown referring to them in questions was not evidence.

4. Badgering

Although many reported decisions contain passing acknowledgements that it is impermissible to badger a witness,[8] there does not appear to have been any judicial attempt to categorize or define the characteristics of unacceptable cross-examination in this regard.

---

[4] (1989), 33 O.A.C. 1 (Ont. C.A.), leave to appeal refused (1989), 37 O.A.C. 318 (note) (S.C.C.).

[5] *Ibid.*, at 6.

[6] *R. v. Snow* (2004), [2004] O.J. No. 4309, 2004 CarswellOnt 4287 (Ont. C.A.) at para. 25.

[7] (2001), [2001] N.S.J. No. 75, 2001 CarswellNS 72 (N.S. C.A.).

[8] See, for example, *R. v. Codina* (1995), 77 O.A.C. 180 (N.S. C.A.) at 196, leave to appeal refused (1995), 30 Imm. L.R. (2d) 248n (S.C.C.).

5. Compound

Compound questions are objectionable.[9]

6. Leading

The seminal judgment on leading questions in Canada is that of Beck J. in *Maves v. Grand Trunk Pacific Railway*:[10]

> I find the general subject of leading questions dealt with in a most satisfactory way in *Best on Evidence*, 11th ed., 624 *et seq.* I quote, italicising what I wish to emphasize:—

>> The chief rule of practice relative to the interrogation of witnesses is that which prohibits "*leading questions*" *i.e., questions which directly or indirectly suggest to the witness the answer he is to give. The rule is, that on material points* a party must not lead his own witnesses, but may lead those of his adversary; in other words, that leading questions are allowed in cross-examination, but not in examination-in-chief. This seems based on two reasons: first, and principally, on the supposition that the witness has a bias in favour of the party bringing him forward, and hostile to his opponent; secondly, that the party calling a witness has an advantage over his adversary, in knowing beforehand what the witness will prove, or, at least, is expected to prove; and that, consequently, if he were allowed to lead, he might interrogate in such a manner as to extract only so much of the knowledge of the witness as would be favourable to his side, or even put a false gloss upon the whole.

> I think a third reason may be added, namely, that a witness, though intending to be entirely fair and honest may, owing, for example, to lack of education, of exactness of knowledge of the precise meaning of words or of appreciation at the moment of their precise meaning, or of alertness to see that what is implied in the question requires modification, honestly assent to a leading question which fails to express his real meaning, which he would probably have completely expressed if allowed to do so in his own words.

> The author proceeds as follows (*Best on Evidence*, 11th ed., 625):—

---

[9] *P. (W.E.) v. P. (T.P.)* (April 15, 1992), Doc. Winnipeg Centre FD 90-01-21283, [1992] M.J. No. 189 (Man. Q.B.). It may be that although a witness need only answer one question at a time, that with regard to complex subjects, it will be for the witness rather than counsel to say whether a particular question is or is not a compound question: *Geac Canada Ltd. v. Prologic Computer Corp.* (1989), 35 B.C.L.R. (2d) 136 (B.C. S.C.).

[10] (1913), 14 D.L.R. 70 (Alta. S.C.) at 73, Harvey C.J., Scott and Stuart JJ. agreeing "in the main" on this point.

On all matters, however, which are *merely introductory*, and form *no part of the substance of the enquiry*, it is both allowable *and proper* for a party to lead his own witnesses, as otherwise much time would be wasted to no purpose. It is sometimes said that the test of a leading question is, whether an answer to it by "Yes" or "No" would be conclusive upon the matter in issue; but although all such questions undoubtedly come within the rule, it is by no means limited to them. Where "Yes" or "No" would be conclusive on any part of the issue, the question would be equally objectionable; as if, on a traverse of notice of dishonour of a bill of exchange, a witness were led either as to the fact of giving notice, or as to the time when it was given. So leading questions ought not to be put when it is sought to prove material and proximate circumstances. Thus, on an indictment for murder by stabbing, to ask a witness whether he saw the accused, covered with blood and with a knife in his hand, coming away from the corpse, would be in the highest degree improper, though all the facts embodied in this question are consistent with his innocence. In practice, leading questions are often allowed to pass without objection, sometimes by express, and sometimes by tacit, consent. This latter occurs where the questions relate to matters which, though strictly speaking, in issue, the examining counsel is aware are not meant to be contested by the other side; or where the opposing counsel does not think it worth his while to object.

On the other hand, however, very unfounded objections are constantly taken on this ground. A question is objectionable as leading when it suggests the *answer*, not when it merely directs the attention of the witness to the *subject* respecting which he is questioned, *e.g.*, on a question whether A. and B. were partners, it has been held not a leading question to ask if A. has interfered in the business of B.; for even supposing he had, that falls far short of constituting him a partner ... It should never be forgotten that "leading" is a relative, not an absolute term. There is no such thing as "leading" in the abstract — for the identical form of question which would be leading of the grossest kind in one case or state of facts, might be not only unobjectionable, but the very fittest mode of interrogation in another.

So that the *general* rule is that in examining one's own witness, not that no leading questions must be asked, but that *on material points* one must *not* lead his own witness but that on points that are *merely introductory and form no part of the substance* of the inquiry one *should* lead.

Beck J. also noted exceptions to the rule against leading:[11]

To the general rule, as just stated, against leading, there are several well recognized exceptions which the author puts as follows:—

There are some exceptions to the rule against leading. 1. For the purpose of identifying persons or things, the attention of the witness may be directly

---

[11] *Ibid.*, at 75.

pointed to them. 2. Where one witness is called to contradict another as to expressions used by the latter, but which he denies having used, he may be asked directly, "Did the other witness use such and such expressions"? The authorities are not quite agreed as to the reason of this exception; and some strongly contend that the memory of the second witness ought first to be exhausted by his being asked what the other said on the occasion in question. 3. The rule which excludes leading questions being chiefly founded on the assumption that a witness must be taken to have a bias in favour of the party by whom he is called, whenever circumstances shew that this is not the case, and that he is either hostile to that party or unwilling to give evidence, the Judge may, in his discretion, allow the rule to be relaxed. And it would seem that, for the same reason, if the witness shews a strong bias in favour of the cross-examining party, the right of leading him ought to be restrained; but the authorities are not quite clear about this. 4. The rule will be relaxed where the inability of a witness to answer questions put in the regular way obviously arises from defective memory; or, 5. From the complicated nature of the matter as to which he is interrogated.

The law regarding leading questions was also touched upon by the Supreme Court of Canada in the more recent case of *R. v. Coffin*,[12] a case in which the trial judge, having come to the conclusion that the witness was not hostile in the legal sense and having therefore refused to permit her to be cross-examined, was nevertheless found to be entitled, in his discretion, to permit leading questions to be put:[13]

> ...while, as a general rule, a party may not either in direct or re-examination put leading questions, the Court has a discretion, not open to review, to relax it whenever it is considered necessary in the interests of justice, as the learned Judge appears to have considered was the situation in the case at bar: *Ex p. Bottomley*, [1909] 2 K.B. 14 at pp. 21-3; *Lawder v. Lawder* (1855), 5 I.C.L.R. 27 at p. 38.

Another issue which has sometimes arisen is whether or not it is permissible for a trial judge to ask leading questions, as in *Squires v. Corner Brook Pulp & Paper Ltd.*:[14]

> Of course, a trial judge is not prohibited from asking leading questions of a witness. See: *Connor v. Township of Brant* (1914), 31 O.L.R. 274 (S.C. App.Div.).

---

[12] (1956), 114 C.C.C. 1 (S.C.C.).
[13] *Ibid.*, at 22, per Kerwin C.J.C.
[14] (1999), [1999] N.J. No. 146, 1999 CarswellNfld 142 (Nfld. C.A.).

7. Personal Opinion of Counsel

Counsel must avoid expressing personal opinion, both in framing questions and in making argument. As noted by the majority. in *R. v. Finta*:[15]

> In our view neither Crown nor defence counsel is entitled to express his personal opinion about a witness, an issue, the basis upon which the prosecution was commenced, or the case in general. Counsel's opinion is not relevant.

The Supreme Court of Canada has commented specifically on the obligation of counsel not to express personal opinion on the guilt or innocence of an accused in *R. v. Boucher*.[16] The Court has also stated that counsel should not express personal opinion on the veracity of a witness in *R. v. Chambers*.[17]

8. Re-examination Raising New Matters

Cory J. noted in *R. v. Evans*[18] that:

> Generally speaking, the right to re-examine must be confined to matters arising from the cross-examination. As a general rule new facts cannot be introduced in re-examination.

9. Repetitive

Repetitive questions are objectionable.[19]

10. Speculative

Speculative questions are objectionable.[20]

---

[15] (1992), 92 D.L.R. (4th) 1 (Ont. C.A.) at 118, affirmed (1994), 112 D.L.R. (4th) (S.C.C.), reconsideration refused (June 23, 1994), Doc. 23023, 23097 (S.C.C.).

[16] (1954), (sub nom. *Boucher v. R.*) 110 C.C.C. 263 (S.C.C.) at 273, per Locke J. and at 278, per Cartwright J.

[17] [1990] 2 S.C.R. 1293 (S.C.C.).

[18] [1993] 2 S.C.R. 629 (S.C.C.) at 644.

[19] *Ortega* and *Parkridge Homes*, *supra,* note 3.

[20] *Allarco Broadcasting Ltd. v. Duke* (1981), [1981] B.C.J. No. 1707, 1981 CarswellBC 374 (B.C. S.C.).

11. Unsupported Allegation

The making of an allegation in cross-examination when counsel cannot support the allegation if it is denied by the witness is a common practice. The value of this tactic has been judicially noted:[21]

> It is not uncommon for counsel to believe what is in fact true, without being able to prove it *otherwise than by cross-examination*; nor is it uncommon for reticent witnesses to concede suggested facts—in the mistaken belief that they are already known to the cross-examiner and will therefore, in any event, emerge.

In Canada, however, the practice was controversial for many years, until the Supreme Court of Canada recently clarified the law and explicitly approved it. Authority for the practice had originally been found in *Fox v. General Medical Council*,[22] where it was held that counsel had acted properly in asking a physician in disciplinary proceedings about his seduction of a patient, despite not subsequently leading any evidence to establish that there had been such a seduction. Lord Radcliffe stated:[23]

> An advocate is entitled to use his discretion as to whether to put questions in the course of cross-examination which are based on material which he is not in a position to prove directly. The penalty is that, if he gets a denial or some answer that does not suit him, the answer stands against him for what it is worth."

This passage from *Fox* was quoted with approval in *R. v. Bencardino*,[24] a case in which a Crown witness was alleged to be changing his testimony as a result of threats made against him in prison. That allegation had been put to the witness by Crown counsel, and despite no evidence subsequently being produced by the Crown to substantiate the allegation, the question was held to be proper.

A more restrictive view appeared to be indicated in *R. v. Howard*.[25] The Crown wished to put to the Defendant's expert the question of whether knowing that Howard's co-accused had pled guilty after the expert's original testimony was delivered would affect the opinion he had given. Lamer J. stated:[26]

---

[21] *R. v. Lyttle*, 2004 SCC 5 (S.C.C.) at para. 47.
[22] [1960] 1 W.L.R. 1017 (Eng. P.C.).
[23] *Ibid.*, at 1023.
[24] (1973), 15 C.C.C. (2d) 342 (Ont. C.A.) at 346.
[25] [1989] 1 S.C.R. 1337 (S.C.C.).
[26] *Ibid.*, at 1347.

> The fact that Trudel had pleaded guilty and had acknowledged that the footprint
> was his was not at the time the question was intended to be put to the expert, and
> was not going to become, a fact adduced in evidence; nor was it a fact that could
> fairly be inferred from the facts in evidence. It is not open to the examiner or
> cross-examiner to put as a fact, or even a hypothetical fact, that which is not and
> will not become part of the case as admissible evidence. On this ground alone,
> the question should have been denied.

Did *Howard* overrule *Fox*? Some courts, such as the Manitoba Court of
Queen's Bench in *R. v. Evans*,[27] found that it did. Others, such as the
Ontario Court of Appeal in *R. v. Jackson*,[28] found otherwise. The decision of the Supreme Court of Canada in *R. v. Chambers*[29] should at least
have made it clear that its earlier decision in *Howard* should not be
interpreted as an absolute prohibition against asking questions which
counsel cannot prove, but confusion obviously remained.

This confusion was eventually manifested at trial in *R. v. Lyttle*.[30]
In that case, a man who had beaten by a gang armed with baseball bats
claimed that he was attacked over a gold chain and identified the defendant as one of his attackers. Defendant's counsel, however, wanted to
raise the possibility that he was really beaten in connection with a drug
deal, a possibility adverted to in police reports, and that he had delib-
erately identified the defendant rather than his real attackers in order to
protect the real attackers, his associates in the drug ring. The trial judge,
however, purporting to rely on *Howard*, refused to allow this line of
cross-examination without an undertaking from the defendant's counsel
to lead supporting evidence. The defendant was prejudiced in the result.

In ruling that the trial judge had erred, the Supreme Court of Canada
first stressed the importance of cross-examination, "particularly, though
of course not exclusively, in the context of a criminal trial."[31] The Court
also noted that "Commensurate with its importance, the right to cross-
examine is now recognized as being protected by ss. 7 and 11(*d*) of the
Canadian Charter of Rights and Freedoms."[32] The Court then stated the
correct law on this topic:[33]

> Unlike the trial judge, and with respect, we believe that a question can be put to
> a witness in cross-examination regarding matters that need not be proved inde-

---

[27] (1994), 1994 CarswellMan 269 (Man. Q.B.).
[28] (1991), 68 C.C.C. (3d) 385 (Ont. C.A.), affirmed (1993), 86 C.C.C. (3d) 385 (S.C.C.), per
Doherty J.A.
[29] *Supra*, note 17.
[30] *Supra*, note 21.
[31] *Ibid.*, at para. 42.
[32] *Ibid.*, at para. 43.
[33] *Ibid.*, at paras. 47-8.

pendently, provided that counsel has a good faith basis for putting the question. It is not uncommon for counsel to believe what is in fact true, without being able to prove it <u>otherwise than by cross-examination</u>; nor is it uncommon for reticent witnesses to concede suggested facts—in the mistaken belief that they are already known to the cross-examiner and will therefore, in any event, emerge.

In this context, a "good faith basis" is a function of the information available to the cross-examiner, his or her belief in its likely accuracy, and the purpose for which it is used. Information falling short of admissible evidence may be put to the witness. In fact, the information may be incomplete or uncertain, provided the cross-examiner does not put suggestions to the witness recklessly or that he or she knows to be false. The cross-examiner may pursue any hypothesis that is honestly advanced on the strength of reasonable inference, experience or intuition. The purpose of the question must be consistent with the lawyer's role as an officer of the court: to suggest what counsel genuinely thinks possible on known facts or reasonable assumptions is in our view permissible; to assert or to imply in a manner that is calculated to mislead is in our view improper and prohibited.

Recognizing that there may be instances in which judges will doubt that counsel possess the requisite "good faith basis" for their questions, the Court also suggested how to proceed in that circumstance:[34]

Where a question implies the existence of a disputed factual predicate that is manifestly tenuous or suspect, a trial judge may properly take appropriate steps, by conducting a *voir dire* or otherwise, to seek and obtain counsel's assurance that a good faith basis exists for putting the question. If the judge is satisfied in this regard and the question is not otherwise prohibited, counsel should be permitted to put the question to the witness.

It can only be hoped that the decision in *Lyttle* will finally put any doubts about the scope of allowable cross-examination to rest.

---

[34] *Ibid.*, at para. 52.

7

IS THERE A PROBLEM WITH THE QUESTIONER?

1. The Role of the Judge

The appropriate role of trial judges in examining witnesses was reviewed in the leading case of *R. v. Brouillard*.[1] In that case, the trial judge had interrupted the testimony of the defence witness more than ten times and asked her more than sixty questions, and had interrupted the testimony of the accused almost twenty times, asking more questions than both counsel. In the following excerpt, Lamer J. quotes from several of the leading cases:[2]

> First of all, it is clear that judges are no longer required to be as passive as they once were; to be what I call sphinx judges. We now not only accept that a judge may intervene in the adversarial debate, but also believe that it is sometimes essential for him to do so for justice in fact to be done. Thus a judge may and sometimes must ask witnesses questions, interrupt them in their testimony and if necessary call them to order.

> One of the decisions most often cited in support of this rule is *Jones v. National Coal Board*, [1957] 2 All E.R. 155. Lord Denning stated the following, at pp. 158-9:

>> No one can doubt that the judge, in intervening as he did, was actuated by the best motives. He was anxious to understand the details of this complicated case, and asked questions to get them clear in his mind. He was anxious that the witnesses should not be harassed unduly in cross-examination, and intervened to protect them when he thought necessary. He was anxious to investigate all the various criticisms that had been made against the board, and to see whether they were well founded or not. Hence he took them up himself with the witnesses from time to time. He was anxious that the case should not be dragged on too long, and intimated clearly when he thought that a point had been sufficiently explored. All those are worthy motives on which judges daily intervene in the conduct of cases and have done for centuries.

---

[1] (sub nom. *Brouillard c. R.*) [1985] 1 S.C.R. 39 (S.C.C.).

[2] *Ibid.* at 44-8.

Nevertheless, we are quite clear that the interventions, taken together, were far more than they should have been. In the system of trial which we have evolved in this country, the judge sits to hear and determine the issues raised by the parties, not to conduct an investigation or examination on behalf of society at large, as happens, we believe, in some foreign countries. Even in England, however, a judge is not a mere umpire to answer the question "How's that?" His object above all is to find out the truth, and to do justice according to law...

More recently, in Canada, in *R. v. Torbiak and Campbell* (1974), 18 C.C.C. (2d) 229 at pp. 230-1, 26 C.R.N.S. 108 at pp. 109-10, which involved a problem similar to the one in the case at bar, the Ontario Court of Appeal stated the following:

The proper conduct of a trial Judge is circumscribed by two considerations. On the one hand his position is one of great power and prestige which gives his every word an especial significance. The position of established neutrality requires that the trial judge should confine himself as much as possible to his own responsibilities and leave to counsel and members of the jury their respective functions. On the other hand his responsibility for the conduct of the trial may well require him to ask questions which ought to be asked and have not been asked on account of the failure of counsel, and so to compel him to interject himself into the examination of witnesses to a degree which he might not otherwise choose.

Since the limits of the allowable conduct are not absolute, but relative to the facts and circumstances of the particular trial within which they are to be observed, every alleged departure during a trial from the accepted standards of judicial conduct must be examined with respect to its effect on the fairness of the trial.

Another illustration of the precept is to be found in the remarks of Lord Greene M.R. in *Yuill v. Yuill*, [1945] 1 All E.R. 183 at p. 185:

It is, of course, always proper for a judge — and it is his duty — to put questions with a view to elucidating an obscure answer or when he thinks that the witness has misunderstood a question put to him by counsel. If there are matters which the judge considers have not been sufficiently cleared up or questions which he himself thinks ought to have been put, he can, of course, take steps to see that the deficiency is made good. It is, I think, generally more convenient to do this when counsel has finished his questions or is passing to a new subject. It must always be borne in mind that the judge does not know what is in counsel's brief and has not the same facilities as counsel for an effective examination-in-chief or cross-examination. In cross-examination, for instance, experienced counsel will see just as clearly as the judge that, for example, a particular question will be a crucial one. But it is for counsel to decide at what stage he will put the question, and the whole strength of the cross-examination may be destroyed if the judge, in his desire to get to what seems to him to be the crucial point, himself intervenes and prematurely puts the question himself.

Finally, I cite with approval the judgment to which the respondent Crown referred us in *R. v. Darlyn* (1946), 88 C.C.C. 269 at p. 277, [1947] 3 D.L.R. 480 at pp. 487-8, 3 C.R. 13, where Bird J.A. wrote the following on behalf of the British Columbia Court of Appeal:

> The nature and extent of a Judge's participation in the examination of a witness is no doubt a matter within his discretion, a discretion which must be exercised judicially. I conceive it to be the function of the Judge to keep the scales of justice in even balance between the Crown and the accused. There can be no doubt in my opinion that a Judge has not only the right, but also the duty to put questions to a witness in order to clarify an obscure answer or to resolve possible misunderstanding of any question by a witness, even to remedy an omission of counsel, by putting questions which the Judge thinks out to have been asked in order to bring out or explain relevant matters...

In short, everyone agrees that a judge has a right and, where necessary, a duty to ask questions, but also that there are certain definite limits on this right. On this point respondent cited the remarks of Humphreys J. in *R. v. Bateman* (1946), 31 Cr. App. R. 106, where he stated [at p. 111]:

> Judges are entitled, if they form the opinion that a witness *is not trying to help the Court*, to do what counsel cannot do, and say: "You behave yourself and tell me the truth." It is sometimes very useful to be able to say that. Sometimes it pulls a witness together and makes him say what is the truth, but, of course, it must not be done until the witness has given some indication that he or she is not trying to tell the truth.

(Emphasis added)

The judge may on occasion call to order a witness who is obviously trying to avoid testifying, who "is not trying to help the court". In *Bateman* a witness said she was not able to recall dates or times accurately. The appellate judges disapproved of the reprimand the commissioner presiding at the trial had given her in the following terms, at pp. 110-1:

> For some reason the Commissioner, who was presiding at the trial, formed the opinion that the witness could give much more satisfactory evidence if she liked, and he cross-examined her and treated her as if she were a thoroughly disreputable liar. It must not be forgotten by those who preside at criminal trials that witnesses, whether called for the prosecution or the defence, are entitled to be treated with courtesy and politeness unless and until they show some symptom of refusing to assist the Court by giving evidence promptly and properly. With all due respect to the Commissioner, it is not the duty of any presiding Judge, as soon as a witness says: "I cannot tell you with accuracy what time something happened", to say: "Oh, yes,

you can. You be careful", or anything designed to force the witness to say something which she really cannot say. The result was that when that cross-examination was taken up to some extent by counsel for the prosecution, this unfortunate woman was induced to give about seven or eight different times as being very probably the times when the appellant went there. Mr. Gordon, who appeared for the appellant, has told us that in the result — and this agrees with our own reading of the transcript — the witness showed herself to be the sort of woman who, if sufficiently badgered, would say anything. It means, not that the woman was not trying to tell the truth, but that she was a person who could not fix times and whose evidence was valueless.

It was only further on that they added the remarks cited by the Crown, and then, by way of clarification, at pp. 111-2:

The mere fact that a witness cannot fix a time is no reason for treating her in that way, and why it was thought necessary so to treat the witnesses in this case is a little difficult to understand.

The observations which were made in *Gilson and Cohen* (1944), 29 Cr. App. R. 174 at p. 181, in which the Court adopted the language of a previous decision, *Cain* (1936), 25 Cr. App. R. 204, at p. 205, are apposite in this case. The observations were to this effect: "There is no question why the Judge should not from time to time interpose such questions as seem to him fair and proper. It was, however, undesirable that...the Judge should proceed, without giving much opportunity to counsel for the defence to interpose, and long before the time had arrived for cross-examination, to cross-examine [the witness] with some severity. The Court agrees with the contention that that was an unfortunate method of conducting the case. It is undesirable that during an examination-in-chief the Judge should appear to be not so much assisting the defence as throwing his weight on the side of the prosecution by cross-examining a prisoner." We would adopt those observations and apply them to any witness, whether called by the prosecution or the defence.

The remarks of Humphreys J. were cited out of context, and the *Bateman* decision as a whole seems somewhat contrary and even fatal to the Crown's position.

Finally, prudence and the resulting judicial restraint must be all the greater where the accused is a witness. He must be allowed to proceed, within limits, of course, but always bearing in mind that at the end of the day he is the only one who may be leaving the court in handcuffs.

In conclusion, although the judge may and must intervene for justice to be done, he must none the less do so in such a way that justice *is seen to be done*. It is all a question of manner.

The prospect of objecting to questions asked by an overly interventionist judge will normally be a daunting one for counsel. Even if it is only to lay the basis for a later appeal, however, such objections must sometimes be made.

8

IS IT TOO LATE TO INTRODUCE NEW EVIDENCE?

1. Rebuttal Evidence

Normally, the party that opens a case — the plaintiff in a civil trial or the Crown in a criminal prosecution — presents all of its evidence first, followed by the other side — the defendant — presenting all of its evidence. To allow the party that opens to present some of its evidence later would result in "splitting the case". There are, however, circumstances in which the Crown or a plaintiff will be allowed to adduce further evidence after the other side has introduced evidence. The first of these is in the case of rebuttal or reply evidence. The law respecting rebuttal evidence was set out by McIntyre J. in *R. v. Krause*:[1]

> At the outset, it may be observed that the law relating to the calling of rebuttal evidence in criminal cases derived originally from, and remains generally consistent with, the rules of law and practice governing the procedures followed in civil and criminal trials. The general rule is that the Crown, or in civil matters the plaintiff, will not be allowed to split its case. The Crown or the plaintiff must produce and enter in its own case all the clearly relevant evidence it has, or that it intends to rely upon, to establish its case with respect to all the issues raised in the pleadings; in a criminal case the indictment and any particulars: see *R. v. Bruno* (1975), 27 C.C.C. (2d) 318 (Ont. C.A.), per Mackinnon J.A., at p. 320, and for a civil case see: *Allcock Laight & Westwood Ltd. v. Patten, Bernard and Dynamic Displays Ltd.*, [1967] 1 O.R. 18 (Ont. C.A.), per Schroeder J.A., at pp. 21-22. This rule prevents unfair surprise, prejudice and confusion which could result if the Crown or the plaintiff were allowed to split its case, that is, to put in part of its evidence — as much as it deemed necessary at the outset — then to close the case and after the defence is complete to add further evidence to bolster the position originally advanced. The underlying reason for this rule is that the defendant or the accused is entitled at the close of the Crown's case to have before it the full case for the Crown so that it is known from the outset what must be met in response.

---

[1] [1986] 2 S.C.R. 466 (S.C.C.) at 473-4.

The plaintiff or the Crown may be allowed to call evidence in rebuttal after completion of the defence case, where the defence has raised some new matter or defence which the Crown has had no opportunity to deal with and which the Crown or the plaintiff could not reasonably have anticipated. But rebuttal will not be permitted regarding matters which merely confirm or reinforce earlier evidence adduced in the Crown's case which could have been brought before the defence was made. It will be permitted only when it is necessary to insure that at the end of the day each party will have had an equal opportunity to hear and respond to the full submissions of the other.

McIntyre J. added the following comments regarding the rule against rebuttal on collateral issues:[2]

Where something new emerges in cross-examination, which is new in the sense that the Crown had no chance to deal with it in its case-in-chief (*i.e.*, there was no reason for the Crown to anticipate that the matter would arise), and where the matter is concerned with the merits of the case (*i.e.*, it concerns an issue essential for the determination of the case) then the Crown may be allowed to call evidence in rebuttal. Where, however, the new matter is collateral, that is, not determinative of an issue arising in the pleadings or indictment or not relevant to matters which must be proved for the determination of the case, no rebuttal will be allowed.

2. Reopening a Case

The distinction between rebuttal evidence and the reopening of a case was addressed by Cory J. in *R. v. G. (S.G.)*:[3]

The rule against "splitting the case" developed primarily in the context of applications to adduce rebuttal evidence by the Crown. Applications to adduce rebuttal evidence and to reopen the case are "close cousins", but not "identical twins": *R. v. F.S.M.* (1996), 93 O.A.C. 201, at p. 208. Rebuttal evidence is properly admissible where the matter addressed arises out of the defence's case, where it is not collateral, and generally, where the Crown could not have foreseen its development: *R. v. Krause*, [1986] 2 S.C.R. 466, at p. 474; *R. v. Aalders*, [1993] 2 S.C.R. 482, at pp. 497-98. With rebuttal evidence, it is the rules of the adversarial process that justify the admission of the reply evidence. In an application to reopen, the Crown is required to establish that the evidence is material to an issue that is properly part of the Crown's case. In order to succeed, the Crown must also explain why the evidence was not led earlier and must justify this departure from the normal rules of the adversarial process. See *F.S.M.*, *supra*, at p. 208.

---

[2] *Ibid.*, at 474.
[3] [1997] 2 S.C.R. 716 (S.C.C.) at 737.

The circumstances in which the Crown can reopen its case in a criminal prosecution were set out by Lamer C.J. for the majority in *R. v. P. (M.B.)*:[4]

> The keystone principle in determining whether the Crown should be allowed to reopen its case has always been whether the accused will suffer prejudice in the legal sense — that is, will be prejudiced in his or her defence. A trial judge's exercise of discretion to permit the Crown's case to be reopened must be exercised judicially and should be based on ensuring that the interests of justice are served.
>
> Traditionally, courts in Canada and in England have treated the stage reached in a proceeding as correlative to prejudice and injustice to the accused. That is, a court's discretion with respect to reopening will be exercised less readily as the trial proceeds. The point is illustrated by taking the following three stages in a trial:
> (1) before the Crown closes its case,
> (2) immediately after the Crown closes its case but before the defence elects whether or not to call evidence (most commonly, this is where the defence has moved for a directed verdict of acquittal for failure by the Crown to prove some essential ingredient of its case), and
> (3) after the defence has started to answer the case against it by disclosing whether or not it will be calling evidence.
>
> In the first phase, before the Crown has closed its case, a trial judge has considerable latitude in exercising his or her discretion to allow the Crown to recall a witness so that his or her earlier testimony can be corrected. Any prejudice to the accused can generally be cured at this early stage by an adjournment, cross-examination of the recalled witness and other Crown witnesses and/or a review by the trial judge of the record in order to determine whether certain portions should be struck.
>
> Once the Crown actually closes its case and the second phase in the proceeding is reached, the trial judge's discretion to allow a reopening will narrow and the corresponding burden on the Crown to satisfy the court that there are no unfair consequences will heighten. The test to be applied by the trial judge is generally understood to be that reopening is to be permitted to correct some oversight or inadvertent omission by the Crown in the presentation of its case, provided of course that justice requires it and there will be no prejudice to the defence.
>
> Lastly, in the third phase after the Crown has closed its case and the defence has started to answer the case against it (or, as in much of the case law, the defence has actually closed its case), a court's discretion is very restricted and is far less likely to be exercised in favour of the Crown. It will only be in the narrowest of circumstances that the Crown will be permitted to reopen its case. Traditionally, an *ex improviso* limitation was said to apply to this stage of the proceeding; that

---

[4] [1994] 1 S.C.R. 555 (S.C.C.) at 568-70.

is, the Crown was only allowed to reopen if some matter arose which no human ingenuity could have foreseen. At this late stage, the question of what "justice" requires will be directed much more to protecting the interests of the accused than to serving the often wider societal interests represented by the Crown, the latter being a more pressing consideration at the first and, to a lesser extent, the second phase.

3. Fresh Evidence on Appeal

That it will sometimes be necessary to adduce additional evidence on appeal is recognized in, for example, the existence of s. 683(1)(d) of the *Criminal Code*, which provides an appellate court with the discretion to admit fresh evidence where it considers it in the interests of justice. McIntyre J. considered that provision in *R. v. Palmer*[5] and identified the following four criteria for the admission of new evidence on appeal:[6]

> (1) The evidence should generally not be admitted if, by due diligence, it could have been adduced at trial provided that this general principle will not be applied as strictly in a criminal case as in civil cases: see *McMartin v. The Queen* [[1964] S.C.R. 484].
> (2) The evidence must be relevant in the sense that it bears upon a decisive or potentially decisive issue in the trial.
> (3) The evidence must be credible in the sense that it is reasonably capable of belief, and
> (4) It must be such that if believed it could reasonably, when taken with the other evidence adduced at trial, be expected to have affected the result.

The Supreme Court of Canada[7] approved the following description of the way these principles interact from *R. v. M. (P.S.)*:[8]

> The last three criteria are conditions precedent to the admission of evidence on appeal. Indeed, the second and third form part of the broader qualitative analysis required by the fourth consideration. The first criterion, due diligence, is not a condition precedent to the admissibility of "fresh" evidence in criminal appeals, but is a factor to be considered in deciding whether the interests of justice warrant the admission of the evidence....

---

[5] (1979), [1980] 1 S.C.R. 759 (S.C.C.).

[6] *Ibid.*, at 775.

[7] *R. v. Lévesque* (2000), [2000] S.C.J. No. 47, 2000 CarswellQue 1994, 2000 CarswellQue 1995 (S.C.C.).

[8] (1992), 77 C.C.C. (3d) 402 (Ont. C.A.) at 410, per Doherty J.A.

In *R. v. Lévesque*,[9] the Supreme Court of Canada considered whether the criteria that apply are the same for both appeals from a verdict and appeals from a sentence. Gonthier J. for the majority ruled:[10]

> I therefore find that the criteria set out in *Palmer* are applicable to applications to tender fresh evidence in an appeal from a sentence.

Note, however, that adducing additional evidence on appeal does not always mean adducing "fresh" evidence in the sense that that term was used in *Palmer*. In *United States v. Shulman*,[11] Arbour J. for the Court pointed out that the evidence required to support the appellant's *Charter* claim could only be raised for the first time in the Court of Appeal, after the Minister had made the decision to surrender and upon judicial review of that decision. This illustrates the need to be mindful of the context and the purpose for which evidence is tendered on appeal.

The burden of satisfying a court that new evidence should be adduced, whether on appeal, in rebuttal, or by reopening, is a heavy one. In seeking to adduce fresh evidence on appeal, counsel will, at least, usually have generous time available for marshalling arguments, a circumstance which distinguishes that situation from all of the others that give rise to arguments on evidentiary issues considered in this volume.

---

[9] *Supra,* note 7.

[10] *Ibid.*, at [CarswellQue 1994] para. 22.

[11] 2001 SCC 21 (S.C.C.), reconsideration refused (2001), 2001 CarswellOnt 2045 (S.C.C.), at paras. 43-6.

Appendix

Canada Evidence Act

An Act respecting Witnesses and Evidence

R.S.C. 1985, c. C-5, as am.R.S.C. 1985, c. 27 (1st Supp.), s. 203; R.S.C. 1985, c. 19 (3rd Supp.), ss. 17, 18; S.C. 1992, c. 1, s. 142 (Sched. V, item 9); 1992, c. 47, s. 66; 1993, c. 28, s. 78 (Sched. III, item 8); 1993, c. 34, s. 15; 1994, c. 44, ss. 85–93; 1995, c. 28, s. 47; 1997, c. 18, ss. 116–118; 1998, c. 9, s. 1; 1999, c. 18, ss. 89–91; 1999, c. 28, ss. 149, 150; 2000, c. 5, ss. 52–57; 2001, c. 41, ss. 43, 44 (Sched. 2), 124, 140, 141(1), (3)–(7); 2002, c. 1, s. 166; 2002, c. 7, s. 96; 2002, c. 8, ss. 118, 19, 183(1)(b) [s. 119 repealed 2001, c. 41, s. 141(3)(a).]; 2003, c. 22, ss. 104, 105; SOR/2004-19; 2004, c. 12, ss. 18, 19; 2005, c. 32, ss. 26, 27; 2005, c. 46, s. 56 [Not in force at date of publication].

Short Title

1. Short title — This Act may be cited as the *Canada Evidence Act.*

PART I — APPLICATION

2. Application — This Part applies to all criminal proceedings and to all civil proceedings and other matters whatever respecting which Parliament has jurisdiction.

Witnesses

3. Interest or crime — A person is not incompetent to give evidence by reason of interest or crime.

4. (1) Accused and spouse — Every person charged with an offence, and, except as otherwise provided in this section, the wife or husband, as the case may be, of the person so charged, is a competent witness for the defence whether the person so charged is charged solely or jointly with any other person.

(2) Accused and spouse — The wife or husband of a person charged with an offence under subsection 136(1) of the *Youth Criminal Justice Act* or with an offence under any of sections 151, 152, 153, 155 or 159, subsection 160(2) or (3), or sections 170 to 173, 179, 212, 215, 218, 271 to 273, 280 to 283, 291 to 294 or 329 of the *Criminal Code*, or an attempt to commit any such offence, is a competent and compellable witness for the prosecution without the consent of the person charged.

(3) Communications during marriage — No husband is compellable to disclose any communication made to him by his wife during their marriage, and no wife is compellable to disclose any communication made to her by her husband during their marriage.

(4) Offences against young persons — The wife or husband of a person charged with an offence against any of sections 220, 221, 235, 236, 237, 239, 240, 266, 267, 268 or 269 of the Criminal Code where the complainant or victim is under the age of fourteen years is a competent and compellable witness for the prosecution without the consent of the person charged.

(5) Saving — Nothing in this section affects a case where the wife or husband of a person charged with an offence may at common law be called as a witness without the consent of that person.

(6) Failure to testify — The failure of the person charged, or of the wife or husband of such person, to testify shall not be made the subject of comment by the judge or by counsel for the prosecution.

　　　　　　　　R.S. 1985, c. 19 (3rd Supp.), s. 17; 2002, c. 1, s. 166.

5. (1) Incriminating questions — No witness shall be excused from answering any question on the ground that the answer to the question may tend to criminate him, or may tend to establish his liability to a civil proceeding at the instance of the Crown or of any person.

(2) Answer not admissible against witness — Where with respect to any question a witness objects to answer on the ground that his answer may tend to criminate him, or may tend to establish his liability to a civil proceeding at the instance of the Crown or of any person, and if but for this Act, or the Act of any provincial legislature, the witness would therefore have been excused from answering the question, then although the witness is by reason of this Act or the provincial Act compelled to answer, the answer so given shall not be used or admissible in evidence against him in any criminal trial or other criminal proceeding against him thereafter taking place, other than a prosecution for perjury in the giving of that evidence or for the giving of contradictory evidence.

1997, c. 18, s. 116

6. (1) Evidence of person with physical disability — If a witness has difficulty communicating by reason of a physical disability, the court may order that the witness be permitted to give evidence by any means that enables the evidence to intelligible.

(2) Evidence of person with mental disability — If a witness with a mental disability is determined under section 16 to have the capacity to give evidence and difficulty communicating by reason of disability, the court may order that the witness be permitted to give evidence by any means that enables the evidence to be intelligible.

(3) Inquiry — The court may conduct an inquiry to determine if the means by which a witness may be permitted to give evidence under subsection (1) or (2) is necessary and reliable.

1998, c. 9, s. 1

6.1 Identification of accused — For greater certainty, a witness may give evidence as to the identity of an accused whom the witness is able to identify visually or in any other sensory manner.

1998, c. 9, s. 1

7. Expert witnesses — Where, in any trial or other proceeding, criminal or civil, it is intended by the prosecution or the defence, or by any party, to examine as witnesses professional or other experts entitled according to the law or practice to give opinion evidence, not more than five of such witnesses may be called on either side without the leave of the court or judge or person presiding.

8. Handwriting comparison — Comparison of a disputed writing with any writing proved to the satisfaction of the court to be genuine shall be permitted to be made by witnesses, and such writings, and the evidence of witnesses respecting those writings, may be submitted to the court and jury as proof of the genuineness or otherwise of the writing in dispute.

9. (1) Adverse witnesses — A party producing a witness shall not be allowed to impeach his credit by general evidence of bad character, but if the witness, in the opinion of the court, proves adverse, the party may contradict him by other evidence, or, by leave of the court, may prove that the witness made at other times a statement inconsistent with his present testimony, but before the last mentioned proof can be given the circumstances of the supposed statement, sufficient to designate the particular occasion, shall be mentioned to the witness, and he shall be asked whether or not he did make the statement.

(2) Previous statements in writing by witness not proved adverse — Where the party producing a witness alleges that the witness made at other times a statement in writing, reduced to writing, or recorded on audio tape or video tape or otherwise, inconsistent with the witness' present testimony, the court may, without proof that the witness is adverse, grant leave to that party to cross-examine the witness as to the statement and the court may consider the cross-examination in determining whether in the opinion of the court the witness is adverse.

1994, c. 44, s. 85

10. (1) Cross-examination as to previous statements — On any trial a witness may be cross-examined as to previous statements that the witness made in writing, or that have been reduced to writing, or recorded on audio tape or video tape or otherwise, relative to the subject-matter of the case, without the writing being shown to the witness or the witness being given the opportunity to listen to the audio tape or view the video tape or otherwise take cognizance of the statements, but, if it is intended to contradict the witness, the witness' attention must, before the contradictory proof can be given, be called to those parts of the statement that are to be used for the purpose of so contradicting the witness, and the judge, at any time during the trial, may require the production of the writing or tape or other medium for inspection, and thereupon make such use of it for the purposes of the trial as the judge thinks fit.

(2) Deposition of witness in criminal investigation — A deposition of a witness, purporting to have been taken before a justice on the investigation of a criminal charge and to be signed by the witness and the justice, returned to and produced from the custody of the proper officer shall be presumed, in the absence of evidence to the contrary, to have been signed by the witness.

1994, c. 44, s. 86

11. Cross-examination as to previous oral statements — Where a witness, on cross-examination as to a former statement made by him relative to the subject-matter of the case and inconsistent with his present testimony, does not distinctly admit that he did make the statement, proof may be given that he did in fact make it, but before the proof can be given the circumstances of the supposed statement, sufficient to designate the particular occasion, shall be mentioned to the witness, and he shall be asked whether or not he did make the statement.

12. (1) Examination as to previous convictions — A witness may be questioned as to whether the witness has been convicted of any offence, excluding any offence designated as a contravention under the Contraventions Act, but including such an offence where the conviction was entered after a trial on an indictment.

(1.1) Proof of previous convictions — If the witness either denies the fact or refuses to answer, the opposite party may prove the conviction.

(2) How conviction proved — A conviction may be proved by producing

(a) a certificate containing the substance and effect only, omitting the formal part, of the indictment and conviction, if it is for an indictable offence, or a copy of the summary conviction, if it is for an offence punishable on summary conviction, purporting to be signed by the clerk of the court or other officer having the custody of the records of the court in which the conviction, if on indictment, was had, or to which the conviction, if summary, was returned; and
(b) proof of identity.

1992, c. 47, s. 66

Oaths and Solemn Affirmations

13. Who may administer oaths — Every court and judge, and every person having, by law or consent of parties, authority to hear and receive evidence, has power to administer an oath to every witness who is legally called to give evidence before that court, judge or person.

14. (1) Solemn affirmation by witness instead of oath — A person may, instead of taking an oath, make the following solemn affirmation:

I solemnly affirm that the evidence to be given by me shall be the truth, the whole truth and nothing but the truth.

(2) Effect — Where a person makes a solemn affirmation in accordance with subsection (1), his evidence shall be taken and have the same effect as if taken under oath.

1994, c. 44, s. 87

15. (1) Solemn affirmation by deponent — Where a person who is required or who desires to make an affidavit or deposition in a proceeding or on an occasion on which or concerning a matter respecting which an oath is required or is lawful, whether on the taking of office or otherwise, does not wish to take an oath, the court or judge, or other officer or person qualified to take affidavits or depositions, shall permit the person to make a solemn affirmation in the words following, namely, "I, ..., do solemnly affirm, etc.", and that solemn affirmation has the same force and effect as if that person had taken an oath.

(2) Effect — Any witness whose evidence is admitted or who makes a solemn affirmation under this section or section 14 is liable to indictment and punishment for perjury in all respects as if he had been sworn.

1994, c. 44, s. 88

16. (1) Witness whose capacity is in question — If a proposed witness is a person of fourteen years of age or older whose mental capacity is challenged, the court shall, before permitting the person to give evidence, conduct an inquiry to determine

    (a) whether the person understands the nature of an oath or a solemn affirmation; and

    (b) whether the person is able to communicate the evidence.

(2) Testimony under oath or solemn affirmation — A person referred to in subsection (1) who understands the nature of an oath or a solemn affirmation and is able to communicate the evidence shall testify under oath or solemn affirmation.

(3) Testimony on promise to tell truth — A person referred to in subsection (1) who does not understand the nature of an oath or a solemn affirmation but is able to communicate the evidence may, notwithstanding any provision of any Act requiring an oath or a solemn affirmation, testify on promising to tell the truth.

(4) Inability to testify — A person referred to in subsection (1) who neither understands the nature of an oath or a solemn affirmation nor is able to communicate the evidence shall not testify.

(5) Burden as to capacity of witness — A party who challenges the mental capacity of a proposed witness of fourteen years of age or more has the burden of satisfying the court that there is an issue as to the capacity of the proposed witness to testify under an oath or a solemn affirmation.

R.S. 1985, c. 19 (3rd Supp.), s. 18; 1994, c. 44, s. 89; 2005, c. 32, s. 26

16.1 (1) Person under fourteen years of age — A person under fourteen years of age is presumed to have the capacity to testify.

(2) No oath or solemn affirmation — A proposed witness under fourteen years of age shall not take an oath or make a solemn affirmation despite a provision of any Act that requires an oath or a solemn affirmation.

(3) Evidence shall be received — The evidence of a proposed witness under fourteen years of age shall be received if they are able to understand and respond to questions.

(4) Burden as to capacity of witness — A party who challenges the capacity of a proposed witness under fourteen years of age has the burden of satisfying the court that there is an issue as to the capacity of the proposed witness to understand and respond to questions.

(5) Court inquiry — If the court is satisfied that there is an issue as to the capacity of a proposed witness under fourteen years of age to understand and respond to questions, it shall, before permitting them to give evidence, conduct an inquiry to determine whether they are able to understand and respond to questions.

(6) Promise to tell truth —The court shall, before permitting a proposed witness under fourteen years of age to give evidence, require them to promise to tell the truth.

(7) Understanding of promise — No proposed witness under fourteen years of age shall be asked any questions regarding their understanding of the nature of the promise to tell the truth for the purpose of determining whether their evidence shall be received by the court.

(8) Effect — For greater certainty, if the evidence of a witness under fourteen years of age is received by the court, it shall have the same effect as if it were taken under oath.

2005, c. 32, s. 27

Judicial Notice

17. Imperial Acts, etc — Judicial notice shall be taken of all Acts of the Imperial Parliament, of all ordinances made by the Governor in Council, or the lieutenant governor in council of any province or colony that, or some portion of which, now forms or hereafter may form part of Canada, and of all the Acts of the legislature of any such province or colony, whether enacted before or after the passing of the *Constitution Act, 1867*.

18. Acts of Canada — Judicial notice shall be taken of all Acts of Parliament, public or private, without being specially pleaded.

Documentary Evidence

19. Copies by Queen's Printer — Every copy of any Act of Parliament, public or private, published by the Queen's Printer, is evidence of that Act and of its contents, and every copy purporting to be published by the Queen's Printer shall be deemed to be so published, unless the contrary is shown.

2000, c. 5, s. 52

20. Imperial proclamations, etc — Imperial proclamations, orders in council, treaties, orders, warrants, licences, certificates, rules, regulations, or other Imperial official records, Acts or documents may be proved

> (a) in the same manner as they may from time to time be provable in any court in England;
> (b) by the production of a copy of the *Canada Gazette*, or a volume of the Acts of Parliament purporting to contain a copy of the same or a notice thereof; or
> (c) by the production of a copy of them purporting to be published by the Queen's Printer.

2000, c. 5, s. 53

21. Proclamations, etc., of Governor General — Evidence of any proclamation, order, regulation or appointment, made or issued by the Governor General or by the Governor in Council, or by or under the authority of any minister or head of any department of the Government of Canada and evidence of a treaty to which Canada is a party, may be given in all or any of the following ways:

(a) by the production of a copy of the *Canada Gazette*, or a volume of the Acts of Parliament purporting to contain a copy of the treaty, proclamation, order, regulation or appointment or a notice thereof;

(b) by the production of a copy of the proclamation, order, regulation or appointment, purporting to be published by the Queen's Printer;

(c) by the production of a copy of the treaty purporting to be published by the Queen's Printer;

(d) by the production, in the case of any proclamation, order, regulation or appointment made or issued by the Governor General or by the Governor in Council, of a copy or extract purporting to be certified to be true by the clerk or assistant or acting clerk of the Queen's Privy Council for Canada; and

(e) by the production, in the case of any order, regulation or appointment made or issued by or under the authority of any minister or head of a department of the Government of Canada, of a copy or extract purporting to be certified to be true by the minister, by his deputy or acting deputy, or by the secretary or acting secretary of the department over which he presides.

2000, c. 5, s. 54

22. (1) Proclamations, etc., of Lieutenant Governor — Evidence of any proclamation, order, regulation or appointment made or issued by a lieutenant governor or lieutenant governor in council of any province, or by or under the authority of any member of the executive council, being the head of any department of the government of the province, may be given in all or any of the following ways:

(a) by the production of a copy of the official gazette for the province, purporting to contain a copy of the proclamation, order, regulation or appointment, or a notice thereof;

(b) by the production of a copy of the proclamation, order, regulation or appointment purporting to be published by the government or Queen's Printer for the province; and

(c) by the production of a copy or extract of the proclamation, order, regulation or appointment purporting to be certified to be true by the clerk or assistant or acting clerk of the executive council, by the head of any department of the government of a province, or by his deputy or acting deputy, as the case may be.

(2) In the case of the territories — Evidence of any proclamation, order, regulation or appointment made by the Lieutenant Governor or Lieutenant Governor in Council of the Northwest Territories, as constituted prior to September 1, 1905, or by the Commissioner in Council of the North-west Territories or the Legislature of Yukon or the Legislature for Nunavut, may be given by the production of a copy of the *Canada Gazette* purporting to contain a copy of the proclamation, order, regulation or appointment, or a notice thereof.

2000, c. 5, s. 55; 2002, c. 7, s. 96.

23. (1) Evidence of judicial proceedings, etc. — Evidence of any proceeding or record whatever of, in or before any court in Great Britain, the Supreme Court, the Federal Court of Appeal, the Federal Court or the Tax Court of Canada, any court in any province, any court in any British colony or possession or any court of record of the United States, of a state of the United States or of any other foreign country, or before any justice of the peace or coroner in a province, may be given in any action or proceeding by an exemplification or certified copy of the proceeding or record, purporting to be under the seal of the court or under the hand or seal of the justice, coroner or court stenographer, as the case may be, without any proof of the authenticity of the seal or of the signature of the justice, coroner or court stenographer or other proof whatever.

(2) Certificate where court has no seal — Where any court, justice or coroner or court stenographer referred to in subsection (1) has no seal, or so certifies, the evidence may be given by a copy purporting to be certified under the signature of a judge or presiding provincial court judge or of the justice or coroner or court stenographer, without any proof of the authenticity of the signature or other proof whatever.

1993, c. 34, s. 15; 1997, c. 18, s. 117; 2002, c. 8, s. 118.

24. Certified copies — In every case in which the original record could be admitted in evidence,

(a) a copy of any official or public document of Canada or of any province, purporting to be certified under the hand of the proper officer or person in whose custody the official or public document is placed, or

(b) a copy of a document, by-law, rule, regulation or proceeding, or a copy of any entry in any register or other book of any municipal or other corporation, created by charter or Act of Parliament or the legislature of any province, purporting to be certified under the seal of the corporation, and the hand of the presiding officer, clerk or secretary thereof,

is admissible in evidence without proof of the seal of the corporation, or of the signature or official character of the person or persons appearing to have signed it, and without further proof thereof.

25. Books and documents — Where a book or other document is of so public a nature as to be admissible in evidence on its mere production from the proper custody, and no other Act exists that renders its contents provable by means of a copy, a copy thereof or extract therefrom is admissible in evidence in any court of justice or before a person having, by law or by consent of parties, authority to hear, receive and examine evidence, if it is proved that it is a copy or extract purporting to be certified to be true by the officer to whose custody the original has been entrusted.

26. (1) Books kept in offices under government of Canada — A copy of any entry in any book kept in any office or department of the Government of Canada, or in any commission, board or other branch in the federal public administration, shall be admitted as evidence of that entry, and of the matters, transactions and accounts therein recorded, if it is proved by the oath or affidavit of an officer of the office or department, commission, board or other branch in the federal public administration that the book was, at the time of the making of the entry, one of the ordinary books kept in the office, department, commission, board or other branch in the federal public administration, that the entry was made in the usual and ordinary course of business of the office, department, commission, board or other branch in the federal public administration and that the copy is a true copy thereof.

(2) Proof of non-issue of licence or document — Where by any Act of Parliament or regulation made under an Act of Parliament provision is made for the issue by a department, commission, board or other branch in the federal public administration of a licence requisite to the doing or having of any act or thing or for the issue of any other document, an affidavit of an officer of the department, commission, board or other branch in the federal public administration, sworn before any commissioner or other person authorized to take affidavits, setting out that he or she has charge of the appropriate records and that after careful examination and search of those records he or she has been unable to find in any given case that any such licence or other document has been issued, shall be admitted in evidence as proof, in the absence of evidence to the contrary, that in that case no licence or other document has been issued.

(3) Proof of mailing departmental matter — Where by any Act of Parliament or regulation made under an Act of Parliament provision is made for sending by mail any request for information, notice or demand by a department or other branch in the federal public administration, an affidavit of an officer of the department or other branch in the federal public administration, sworn before any commissioner or other person authorized to take affidavits, setting out that he or she has charge of the appropriate records, that he or she has a knowledge of the facts in the particular case, that the request, notice or demand was sent by registered letter on a named date to the person or firm to whom it was addressed (indicating that address) and that he or she identifies as exhibits attached to the affidavit the post office certificate of registration of the letter and a true copy of the request, notice or demand, shall, on production and proof of the post office receipt for the delivery of the registered letter to the addressee, be admitted in evidence as proof, in the absence of evidence to the contrary, of the sending and of the request, notice or demand.

(4) Proof of official character — Where proof is offered by affidavit pursuant to this section it is not necessary to prove the official character of the person making the affidavit if that information is set out in the body of the affidavit.

2003, c. 22, s. 104

27. Notarial acts in Quebec — Any document purporting to be a copy of a notarial act or instrument made, filed or registered in the Province of Quebec, and to be certified by a notary or prothonotary to be a true copy of the original in his possession as such notary or prothonotary, shall be admitted in evidence in the place and stead of the original and has the same force and effect as the original would have if produced and proved, but it may be proved in rebuttal that there is no original, that the copy is not a true copy of the original in some material particular or that the original is not an instrument of such nature as may, by the law of the Province of Quebec, be taken before a notary or be filed, enrolled or registered by a notary in that Province.

28. (1) Notice of production of book or document — No copy of any book or other document shall be admitted in evidence, under the authority of section 23, 24, 25, 26 or 27, on any trial, unless the party intending to produce the copy has before the trial given to the party against whom it is intended to be produced reasonable notice of that intention.

(2) Not less than 7 days — The reasonableness of the notice referred to in subsection (1) shall be determined by the court, judge or other person presiding, but the notice shall not in any case be less than seven days.

29. (1) Copies of entries — Subject to this section, a copy of any entry in any book or record kept in any financial institution shall in all legal proceedings be admitted in evidence as proof, in the absence of evidence to the contrary, of the entry and of the matters, transactions and accounts therein recorded.

(2) Admission in evidence — A copy of an entry in the book or record described in subsection (1) shall not be admitted in evidence under this section unless it is first proved that the book or record was, at the time of the making of the entry, one of the ordinary books or records of the financial institution, that the entry was made in the usual and ordinary course of business, that the book or record is in the custody or control of the financial institution and that the copy is a true copy of it, and such proof may be given by any person employed by the financial institution who has knowledge of the book or record or the manager or accountant of the financial institution, and may be given orally or by affidavit sworn before any commissioner or other person authorized to take affidavits.

(3) Cheques, proof of "no account" — Where a cheque has been drawn on any financial institution or branch thereof by any person, an affidavit of the manager or accountant of the financial institution or branch, sworn before any commissioner or other person authorized to take affidavits, setting out that he is the manager or accountant, that he has made a careful examination and search of the books and records for the purpose of ascertaining whether or not that person has an account with the financial institution or branch and that he has been unable to find such an account, shall be admitted in evidence as proof, in the absence of evidence to the contrary, that that person has no account in the financial institution or branch.

(4) Proof of official character — Where evidence is offered by affidavit pursuant to this section, it is not necessary to prove the signature or official character of the person making the affidavit if the official character of that person is set out in the body of the affidavit.

(5) Compulsion of production or appearance — A financial institution or officer of a financial institution is not in any legal proceedings to which the financial institution is not a party compellable to produce any book or record, the contents of which can be proved under this section, or to appear as a witness to prove the matters, transactions and accounts therein recorded unless by order of the court made for special cause.

(6) Order to inspect and copy — On the application of any party to a legal proceeding, the court may order that that party be at liberty to inspect and take copies of any entries in the books or records of a financial institution for the purposes of the legal proceeding, and the person whose account is to be inspected shall be notified of the application at least two clear days before the hearing thereof, and if it is shown to the satisfaction of the court that he cannot be notified personally, the notice may be given by addressing it to the financial institution.

(7) Warrants to search — Nothing in this section shall be construed as prohibiting any search of the premises of a financial institution under the authority of a warrant to search issued under any other Act of Parliament, but unless the warrant is expressly endorsed by the person under whose hand it is issued as not being limited by this section, the authority conferred by any such warrant to search the premises of a financial institution and to seize and take away anything in it shall, with respect to the books or records of the institution, be construed as limited to the searching of those premises for the purpose of inspecting and taking copies of entries in those books or records, and section 490 of the Criminal Code does not apply in respect of the copies of those books or records obtained under a warrant referred to in this section.

(8) Computation of time — Holidays shall be excluded from the computation of time under this section.

(9) Definitions — In this section,

"court" means the court, judge, arbitrator or person before whom a legal proceeding is held or taken;

"financial institution" means the Bank of Canada, the Business Development Bank of Canada and any institution that accepts in Canada deposits of money from its members or the public, and includes a branch, agency or office of any of those Banks or institutions;

"legal proceeding" means any civil or criminal proceeding or inquiry in which evidence is or may be given, and includes an arbitration.

1994, c. 44, s. 90; 1995, c. 28, s. 47(a); 1999, c. 28, s. 149

30. (1) Business records to be admitted in evidence — Where oral evidence in respect of a matter would be admissible in a legal proceeding, a record made in the usual and ordinary course of business that contains information in respect of that matter is admissible in evidence under this section in the legal proceeding on production of the record.

(2) Inference where information not in business record — Where a record made in the usual and ordinary course of business does not contain information in respect of a matter the occurrence or existence of which might reasonably be expected to be recorded in that record, the court may on production of the record admit the record for the purpose of establishing that fact and may draw the inference that the matter did not occur or exist.

(3) Copy of records — Where it is not possible or reasonably practicable to produce any record described in subsection (1) or (2), a copy of the record accompanied by two documents, one that is made by a person who states why it is not possible or reasonably practicable to produce the record and one that sets out the source from which the copy was made, that attests to the copy's authenticity and that is made by the person who made the copy, is admissible in evidence under this section in the same manner as if it were the original of the record if each document is

(a) an affidavit of each of those persons sworn before a commissioner or other person authorized to take affidavits; or

(b) a certificate or other statement pertaining to the record in which the person attests that the certificate or statement is made in conformity with the laws of a foreign state, whether or not the certificate or statement is in the form of an affidavit attested to before an official of the foreign state.

(4) Where record kept in form requiring explanation — Where production of any record or of a copy of any record described in subsection (1) or (2) would not convey to the court the information contained in the record by reason of its having been kept in a form that requires explanation, a transcript of the explanation of the record or copy prepared by a person qualified to make the explanation is admissible in evidence under this section in the same manner as if it were the original of the record if it is accompanied by a document that sets out the person's qualifications to make the explanation, attests to the accuracy of the explanation, and is

(a) an affidavit of that person sworn before a commissioner or other person authorized to take affidavits; or

(b) a certificate or other statement pertaining to the record in which the person attests that the certificate or statement is made in conformity with the laws of a foreign state, whether or not the certificate or statement is in the form of an affidavit attested to before an official of the foreign state.

(5) Court may order other part of record to be produced — Where part only of a record is produced under this section by any party, the court may examine any other part of the record and direct that, together with the part of the record previously so produced, the whole or any part of the other part thereof be produced by that party as the record produced by him.

(6) Court may examine record and hear evidence — For the purpose of determining whether any provision of this section applies, or for the purpose of determining the probative value, if any, to be given to information contained in any record admitted in evidence under this section, the court may, on production of any record, examine the record, admit any evidence in respect thereof given orally or by affidavit including evidence as to the circumstances in which the information contained in the record was written, recorded, stored or reproduced, and draw any reasonable inference from the form or content of the record.

(7) Notice of intention to produce record or affidavit — Unless the court orders otherwise, no record or affidavit shall be admitted in evidence under this section unless the party producing the record or affidavit has, at least seven days before its production, given notice of his intention to produce it to each other party to the legal proceeding and has, within five days after receiving any notice in that behalf given by any such party, produced it for inspection by that party.

(8) Not necessary to prove signature and official character — Where evidence is offered by affidavit under this section, it is not necessary to prove the signature or official character of the person making the affidavit if the official character of that person is set out in the body of the affidavit.

(9) Examination on record with leave of court — Subject to section 4, any person who has or may reasonably be expected to have knowledge of the making or contents of any record produced or received in evidence under this section may, with leave of the court, be examined or cross-examined thereon by any party to the legal proceeding.

(10) Evidence inadmissible under this section — Nothing in this section renders admissible in evidence in any legal proceeding

    (a) such part of any record as is proved to be
        (i) a record made in the course of an investigation or inquiry,
        (ii) a record made in the course of obtaining or giving legal advice or in contemplation of a legal proceeding.
        (iii) a record in respect of the production of which any privilege exists and is claimed, or
        (iv) a record of or alluding to a statement made by a person who is not, or if he were living and of sound mind would not be, competent and compellable to disclose in the legal proceeding a matter disclosed in the record;
    (b) any record the production of which would be contrary to public policy; or
    (c) any transcript or recording of evidence taken in the course of another legal proceeding.

(11) Construction of this section — The provisions of this section shall be deemed to be in addition to and not in derogation of

(a) any other provision of this or any other Act of Parliament respecting the admissibility in evidence of any record or the proof of any matter; or

(b) any existing rule of law under which any record is admissible in evidence or any matter may be proved.

(12) Definitions — In this section,

"business" means any business, profession, trade, calling, manufacture or undertaking of any kind carried on in Canada or elsewhere whether for profit or otherwise, including any activity or operation carried on or performed in Canada or elsewhere by any government, by any department, branch, board, commission or agency of any government, by any court or other tribunal or by any other body or authority performing a function of government;

"copy" in relation to any record, includes a print, whether enlarged or not, from a photographic film of the record, and **"photographic film"** includes a photographic plate, microphotographic film or photostatic negative;

"court" means the court, judge, arbitrator or person before whom a legal proceeding is held or taken;

"legal proceeding" means any civil or criminal proceeding or inquiry in which evidence is or may be given, and includes an arbitration;

"record" includes the whole or any part of any book, document, paper, card, tape or other thing on or in which information is written, recorded, stored or reproduced, and, except for the purposes of subsections (3) and (4), any copy or transcript admitted in evidence under this section pursuant to subsection (3) or (4).

                                                1994, c. 44, s. 91

31. (1) Definitions — In this section,

"corporation" means any bank, including the Bank of Canada and the Business Development Bank of Canada, any authorized foreign bank within the meaning of section 2 of the *Bank Act* and each of the following carrying on business in Canada, namely, every railway, express, tele-graph and telephone company (except a street railway and tramway company), insurance company or society, trust company and loan company;

"government" means the government of Canada or of any province and includes any department, commission, board or branch of any such government; and

"photographic film" includes any photographic plate, microphoto-graphic film and photostatic negative.

(2) When print admissible in evidence — A print, whether enlarged or not, from any photographic film of

(a) an entry in any book or record kept by any government or corporation and destroyed, lost or delivered to a customer after the film was taken,
(b) any bill of exchange, promissory note, cheque, receipt, instrument or document held by any government or corporation and destroyed, lost or delivered to a customer after the film was taken, or
(c) any record, document, plan, book or paper belonging to or deposited with any government or corporation,

is admissible in evidence in all cases in which and for all purposes for which the object photographed would have been admitted on proof that

(d) while the book, record, bill of exchange, promissory note, cheque, receipt, instrument or document, plan, book or paper was in the custody or control of the government or corporation, the photographic film was taken thereof in order to keep a permanent record thereof, and
(e) the object photographed was subsequently destroyed by or in the presence of one or more of the employees of the government or corporation, or was lost or was delivered to a customer.

(3) Evidence of compliance with conditions — Evidence of compliance with the conditions prescribed by this section may be given by any one or more of the employees of the government or corporation, having knowledge of the taking of the photographic film, of the destruction, loss or delivery to a customer, or of the making of the print, as the case may be, either orally or by affidavit sworn in any part of Canada before any notary public or commissioner for oaths.

(4) Proof by notarial copy — Unless the court otherwise orders, a notarial copy of an affidavit under subsection (3) is admissible in evidence in lieu of the original affidavit.
1992, c. 1, s. 142 (Sched. V, item 9); 1995, c. 28, s. 47(b); 1999, c. 28, s. 150

31.1 Authentication of electronic documents — Any person seeking to admit an electronic document as evidence has the burden of proving its authenticity by evidence capable of supporting a finding that the electronic document is that which it is purported to be.
2000, c. 5, s. 56

31.2 (1) Application of best evidence rule — electronic documents — The best evidence rule in respect of an electronic document is satisfied

(a) on proof of the integrity of the electronic documents system by or in which the electronic document was recorded or stored; or
(b) if an evidentiary presumption established under section 31.4 applies.

(2) Printouts — Despite subsection (1), in the absence of evidence to the contrary, an electronic document in the form of a printout satisfies the best evidence rule if the printout has been manifestly or consistently acted on, relied on or used as a record of the information recorded or stored in the printout.
2000, c. 5, s. 56

31.3 Presumption of integrity — For the purposes of subsection 31.2(1), in the absence of evidence to the contrary, the integrity of an electronic documents system by or in which an electronic document is recorded or stored is proven

(a) by evidence capable of supporting a finding that at all material times the computer system or other similar device used by the electronic documents system was operating properly or, if it was not, the fact of its not operating properly did not affect the integrity of the electronic document and there are no other reasonable grounds to doubt the integrity of the electronic documents system;

(b) if it is established that the electronic document was recorded or stored by a party who is adverse in interest to the party seeking to introduce it; or

(c) if it is established that the electronic document was recorded or stored in the usual and ordinary course of business by a person who is not a party and who did not record or store it under the control of the party seeking to introduce it.

2000, c. 5, s. 56

31.4 Presumptions regarding secure electronic signatures — The Governor in Council may make regulations establishing evidentiary presumptions in relation to electronic documents signed with secure electronic signatures, including regulations respecting

(a) the association of secure electronic signatures with persons; and

(b) the integrity of information contained in electronic documents signed with secure electronic signatures.

2000, c. 5, s. 56

31.5 Standards may be considered — For the purpose of determining under any rule of law whether an electronic document is admissible, evidence may be presented in respect of any standard, procedure, usage or practice concerning the manner in which electronic documents are to be recorded or stored, having regard to the type of business, enterprise or endeavour that used, recorded or stored the electronic document and the nature and purpose of the electronic document.

2000, c. 5, s. 56

31.6 (1) Proof by affidavit — The matters referred to in subsection 31.2(2) and sections 31.3 and 31.5 and in regulations made under section 31.4 may be established by affidavit.

(2) Cross-examination — A party may cross-examine a deponent of an affidavit referred to in subsection (1) that has been introduced in evidence

(a) as of right, if the deponent is an adverse party or is under the control of an adverse party; and

(b) with leave of the court, in the case of any other deponent.

2000, c. 5, s. 56

31.7 Application — Sections 31.1 to 31.4 do not affect any rule of law relating to the admissibility of evidence, except the rules relating to authentication and best evidence.

2000, c. 5, s. 56

31.8 Definitions — The definitions in this section apply in sections 31.1 to 31.6.

"computer system" means a device that, or a group of interconnected or related devices one or more of which,

(a) contains computer programs or other data; and
(b) pursuant to computer programs, performs logic and control, and may perform any other function.

"data" means representations of information or of concepts, in any form.

"electronic document" means data that is recorded or stored on any medium in or by a computer system or other similar device and that can be read or perceived by a person or a computer system or other similar device. It includes a display, printout or other output of that data.

"electronic documents system" includes a computer system or other similar device by or in which data is recorded or stored and any procedures related to the recording or storage of electronic documents.

"secure electronic signature" means a secure electronic signature as defined in subsection 31(1) of the *Personal Information Protection and Electronic Documents Act.*

2000, c. 5, s. 56

32. (1) Order signed by Secretary of State — An order signed by the Secretary of State of Canada and purporting to be written by command of the Governor General shall be admitted in evidence as the order of the Governor General.

(2) Copies published in *Canada Gazette* — All copies of official and other notices, advertisements and documents published in the *Canada Gazette* are admissible in evidence as proof, in the absence of evidence to the contrary, of the originals and of their contents.

2000, c. 5, s. 57

33. (1) Proof of handwriting of person certifying — No proof shall be required of the handwriting or official position of any person certifying, in pursuance of this Act, to the truth of any copy of or extract from any proclamation, order, regulation, appointment, book or other document.

(2) Printed or written — Any copy or extract referred to in subsection (1) may be in print or in writing, or partly in print and partly in writing.

34. (1) Attesting witness — It is not necessary to prove by the attesting witness any instrument to the validity of which attestation is not requisite.

(2) Instrument, how proved — Any instrument referred to in subsection (1) may be proved by admission or otherwise as if there had been no attesting witness thereto.

35. Impounding of forged instrument — Where any instrument that has been forged or fraudulently altered is admitted in evidence, the court or the judge or person who admits the instrument may, at the request of any person against whom it is admitted in evidence, direct that the instrument shall be impounded and be kept in the custody of an officer of the court or other proper person for such period and subject to such conditions as to the court, judge or person admitting the instrument seem meet.

36. Construction — This Part shall be deemed to be in addition to and not in derogation of any powers of proving documents given by any existing Act or existing at law.

Interpretation

[Heading added 2001, c. 41, s. 43.]

36.1 Definition of "official" In sections 37 to 38.16, "official" has the same meaning as in section 118 of the *Criminal Code*.

2001, c. 41, s. 43

Specified Public Interest

[Heading amended 2001, c. 41, s. 43.]

37. (1) Objection to disclosure of information — Subject to sections 38 to 38.16, a Minister of the Crown in right of Canada or other official may object to the disclosure of information before a court, person or body with jurisdiction to compel the production of information by certifying orally or in writing to the court, person or body that the information should not be disclosed on the grounds of a specified public interest.

(1.1) Obligation of court, person or body — If an objection is made under subsection (1), the court, person or body shall ensure that the information is not disclosed other than in accordance with this Act.

(2) Objection made to superior court — If an objection to the disclosure of information is made before a superior court, that court may determine the objection.

(3) Objection not made to superior court — If an objection to the disclosure of information is made before a court, person or body other than a superior court, the objection may be determined, on application, by

    (a) the Federal Court, in the case of a person or body vested with power to compel production by or under an Act of Parliament if the person or body is not a court established under a law of a province; or

    (b) the trial division or trial court of the superior court of the province within which the court, person or body exercises its jurisdiction, in any other case.

(4) Limitation period — An application under subsection (3) shall be made within 10 days after the objection is made or within any further or lesser time that the court having jurisdiction to hear the application considers appropriate in the circumstances.

(4.1) Disclosure order — Unless the court having jurisdiction to hear the application concludes that the disclosure of the information to which the objection was made under subsection (1) would encroach upon a specified public interest, the court may authorize by order the disclosure of the information.

(5) Disclosure order — If the court having jurisdiction to hear the application concludes that the disclosure of the information to which the objection was made under subsection (1) would encroach upon a specified public interest, but that the public interest in disclosure outweighs in importance the specified public interest, the court may, by order, after considering both the public interest in disclosure and the form of and conditions to disclosure that are most likely to limit any encroachment upon the specified public interest resulting from disclosure, authorize the disclosure, subject to any conditions that the court considers appropriate, of all of the information, a part or summary of the information, or a written admission of facts relating to the information.

(6) Prohibition order — If the court does not authorize disclosure under subsection (4.1) or (5), the court shall, by order, prohibit disclosure of the information.

(6.1) Evidence — The court may receive into evidence anything that, in the opinion of the court, is reliable and appropriate, even if it would not otherwise be admissible under Canadian law, and may base its decision on that evidence.

(7) When determination takes effect — An order of the court that authorizes disclosure does not take effect until the time provided or granted to appeal the order, or a judgment of an appeal court that confirms the order, has expired, or no further appeal from a judgment that confirms the order is available.

(8) Introduction into evidence — A person who wishes to introduce into evidence material the disclosure of which is authorized under subsection (5), but who may not be able to do so by reason of the rules of admissibility that apply before the court, person or body with jurisdiction to compel the production of information, may request from the court having jurisdiction under subsection (2) or (3) an order permitting the introduction into evidence of the material in a form or subject to any conditions fixed by that court, as long as that form and those conditions, comply with the order made under subsection (5).

(9) Relevant factors — For the purpose of subsection (8), the court having jurisdiction under subsection (2) or (3) shall consider all the factors that would be relevant for a determination of admissibility before the court, person or body.

2001, c. 41, ss. 43, 140; 2002, c. 8, s. 183(1)(b)

37.1 (1) Appeal to court of appeal — An appeal lies from a determination under any of subsections 37(4.1) to (6)

(a) to the Federal Court of Appeal from a determination of the Federal Court; or

(b) to the court of appeal of a province from a determination of a trial division or trial court of a superior court of the province.

(2) Limitation period for appeal — An appeal under subsection (1) shall be brought within 10 days after the date of the determination appealed from or within any further time that the court having jurisdiction to hear the appeal considers appropriate in the circumstances.

2001, c. 41, ss. 43, 141(3)(b)

37.2 Limitation periods for appeals to Supreme Court of Canada — Notwithstanding any other Act of Parliament,

(a) an application for leave to appeal to the Supreme Court of Canada from a judgment made under subsection 37.1(1) shall be made within 10 days after the date of the judgment appealed from or within any further time that the court having jurisdiction to grant leave to appeal considers appropriate in the circumstances; and

(b) if leave to appeal is granted, the appeal shall be brought in the manner set out in subsection 60(1) of the *Supreme Court Act* but within the time specified by the court that grants leave.

2001, c. 41, s. 43

37.21 [Repealed 2004, c. 12, s. 18.]

37.3 (1) Protection of right to a fair trial — A judge presiding at a criminal trial or other criminal proceeding may make any order that he or she considers appropriate in the circumstances to protect the right of the accused to a fair trial, as long as that order complies with the terms of any order made under any of subsections 37(4.1) to (6) in relation to that trial or proceeding or any judgment made on appeal of an order made under any of those subsections.

(2) Potential orders — The orders that may be made under subsection (1) include, but are not limited to, the following orders:

(a) an order dismissing specified counts of the indictment or information, or permitting the indictment or information to proceed only in respect of a lesser or included offence;

(b) an order effecting a stay of the proceedings; and

(c) an order finding against any party on any issue relating to information the disclosure of which is prohibited.

2001, c. 41, s. 43

International Relations and National Defence and National Security

[Heading added 2001, c. 41, s. 43.]

38. Definitions — The following definitions apply in this section and in sections 38.01 to 38.15.

"judge" means the Chief Justice of the Federal Court or a judge of that Court designated by the Chief Justice to conduct hearings under section 38.04.

"participant" means a person who, in connection with a proceeding, is required to disclose, or expects to disclose or cause the disclosure of, information.

"potentially injurious information" means information of a type that, if it were disclosed to the public, could injure international relations or national defence or national security.

"proceeding" means a proceeding before a court, person or body with jurisdiction to compel the production of information.

"prosecutor" means an agent of the Attorney General of Canada or of the Attorney General of a province, the Director of Military Prosecutions under the *National Defence Act* or an individual who acts as a prosecutor in a proceeding

"sensitive information" means information relating to international relations or national defence or national security that is in the possession of the Government of Canada, whether originating from inside or outside Canada, and is of a type that the Government of Canada is taking measures to safeguard.

2001, c. 41, ss. 43, 141(4)

38.01 (1) Notice to Attorney General of Canada — Every participant who, in connection with a proceeding, is required to disclose, or expects to disclose or cause the disclosure of, information that the participant believes is sensitive information or potentially injurious information shall, as soon as possible, notify, the Attorney General of Canada in writing of the possibility of the disclosure, and of the nature, date and place of the proceeding.

(2) During a proceeding — Every participant who believes that sensitive information or potentially injurious information is about to be disclosed, whether by the participant or another person, in the course of a proceeding shall raise the matter with the person presiding at the proceeding and notify the Attorney General of Canada in writing of the matter as soon as possible, whether or not notice has been given under subsection (1). In such circumstances, the person presiding at the proceeding shall ensure that the information is not disclosed other than in accordance with this Act.

(3) Notice of disclosure from official — An official, other than a participant, who believes that sensitive information or potentially injurious information may be disclosed in connection with a proceeding may notify the Attorney General of Canada in writing of the possibility of the disclosure, and of the nature, date and place of the proceeding.

(4) During a proceeding — An official, other than a participant, who believes that sensitive information or potentially injurious information is about to be disclosed in the course of a proceeding may raise the matter with the person presiding at the proceeding. If the official raises the matter, he or she shall notify the Attorney General of Canada in writing of the matter as soon as possible, whether or not notice has been given under subsection (3), and the person presiding at the proceeding shall ensure that the information is not disclosed other than in accordance with this Act.

(5) Military proceedings — In the case of a proceeding under Part III of the *National Defence Act*, notice under any of subsections (1) to (4) shall be given to both the Attorney General of Canada and the Minister of National Defence.

(6) Exception — This section does not apply when

(a) the information is disclosed by a person to their solicitor in connection with a proceeding, if the information is relevant to that proceeding;

(b) the information is disclosed to enable the Attorney General of Canada, the Minister of National Defence, a judge or a court hearing an appeal from, or a review of, an order of the judge to discharge their responsibilities under section 38, this section and sections 38.02 to 38.13, 38.15 and 38.16;

(c) disclosure of the information is authorized by the government institution in which or for which the information was produced or, if the information was not produced in or for a government institution, the government institution in which it was first received; or

(d) the information is disclosed to an entity and, where applicable, for a purpose listed in the schedule.

(7) Exception — Subsections (1) and (2) do not apply to a participant if a government institution referred to in paragraph (6)(c) advises the participant that it is not necessary, in order to prevent disclosure of the information referred to in that paragraph, to give notice to the Attorney General of Canada under subsection (1) or to raise the matter with the person presiding under subsection (2).

(8) Schedule — The Governor in Council may, by order, add to or delete from the schedule a reference to any entity or purpose, or amend such a reference.

2001, c. 41, s. 43

38.02 (1) Disclosure prohibited — Subject to subsection 38.01(6), no person shall disclose in connection with a proceeding

(a) information about which notice is given, under any of subsections 38.01(1) to (4);

(b) the fact that notice is given to the Attorney General of Canada under any of subsections 38.01(1) to (4), or to the Attorney General of Canada and the Minister of National Defence under subsection 38.01(5);

(c) the fact that an application is made to the Federal Court under section 38.04 or that an appeal or review of an order made under any of subsections 38.06(1) to (3) in connection with the application is instituted; or

(d) the fact that an agreement is entered into under section 38.031 or subsection 38.04(6).

(1.1) Entities — When an entity listed in the schedule, for any purpose listed there in relation to that entity, makes a decision or order that would result in the disclosure of sensitive information or potentially injurious information, the entity shall not disclose the information or cause it to be disclosed until notice of intention to disclose the information has been given to the Attorney General of Canada and a period of 10 days has elapsed after notice was given.

(2) Exceptions — Disclosure of the information or the facts referred to in subsection (1) is not prohibited if

(a) the Attorney General of Canada authorizes the disclosure in writing under section 38.03 or by agreement under section 38.031 or subsection 38.04(6); or

(b) a judge authorizes the disclosure under subsection 38.06(1) or (2) or a court hearing an appeal from, or a review of, the order of the judge authorizes the disclosure, and either the time provided to appeal the order or judgment has expired or no further appeal is available.

2001, c. 41, ss. 43, 141(5)

38.03 (1) Authorization by Attorney General of Canada — The Attorney General of Canada may, at any time and subject to any conditions that he or she considers appropriate, authorize the disclosure of all or part of the information and facts the disclosure of which is prohibited under subsection 38.02(1).

(2) Military proceedings — In the case of a proceeding under Part III of the *National Defence Act*, the Attorney General of Canada may authorize disclosure only with the agreement of the Minister of National Defence.

(3) Notice —The Attorney General of Canada shall, within 10 days after the day on which he or she first receives a notice about information under any of subsections 38.01(1) to (4), notify in writing every person who provided notice under section 38.01 about that information of his or her decision with respect to disclosure of the information.

2001, c. 41, s. 43

38.031 (1) Disclosure agreement — The Attorney General of Canada and a person who has given notice under subsection 38.01(1) or (2) and is not required to disclose information but wishes, in connection with a proceeding, to disclose any facts referred to in paragraphs 38.02(l)(b) to (d) or information about which he or she gave the notice, or to cause that disclosure, may, before the person applies to the Federal Court under paragraph 38.04(2)(c), enter into an agreement that permits the disclosure of part of the facts or information or disclosure of the facts or information subject to conditions.

(2) No application to Federal Court — If an agreement is entered into under subsection (1), the person may not apply to the Federal Court under paragraph 38.04(2)(c) with respect to the information about which he or she gave notice to the Attorney General of Canada under subsection 38.01(1) or (2).

2001, c. 41, ss. 43, 141(6)

38.04 (1) Application to Federal Court — Attorney General of Canada — The Attorney General of Canada may, at any time and in any circumstances, apply to the Federal Court for an order with respect to the disclosure of information about which notice was given under any of subsections 38.01(1) to (4).

(2) Application to Federal Court — general — If, with respect to information about which notice was given under any of subsections 38.01(1) to (4), the Attorney General of Canada does not provide notice of a decision in accordance with subsection 38.03(3) or, other than by an agreement under section 38.031, authorizes the disclosure of only part of the information or disclosure subject to any conditions,

> (a) the Attorney General of Canada shall apply to the Federal Court for an order with respect to disclosure of the information if a person who gave notice under subsection 38.01 (1) or (2) is a witness;
> (b) a person, other than a witness, who is required to disclose information in connection with a proceeding shall apply to the Federal Court for an order with respect to disclosure of the information; and
> (c) a person who is not required to disclose information in connection with a proceeding but who wishes to disclose it or to cause its

disclosure may apply to the Federal Court for an order with respect to disclosure of the information.

(3) Notice to Attorney General of Canada — A person who applies to the Federal Court under paragraph (2)(b) or (c) shall provide notice of the application to the Attorney General of Canada.

(4) Court records — An application under this section is confidential. Subject to section 38.12, the Chief Administrator of the Courts Administration Service may take any measure that he or she considers appropriate to protect the confidentiality of the application and the information to which it relates.

(5) Procedure — As soon as the Federal Court is seized of an application under this section, the judge

(a) shall hear the representations of the Attorney General of Canada and, in the case of a proceeding under Part III of the *National Defence Act*, the Minister of National Defence, concerning the identity of all parties or witnesses whose interests may be affected by either the prohibition of disclosure or the conditions to which disclosure is subject, and concerning the persons who should be given notice of any hearing of the matter;

(b) shall decide whether it is necessary to hold any hearing of the matter;

(c) if he or she decides that a hearing should be held, shall

(i) determine who should be given notice of the hearing,

(ii) order the Attorney General of Canada to notify those persons, and

(iii) determine the content and form of the notice; and

(d) if he or she considers it appropriate in the circumstances, may give any person the opportunity to make representations.

(6) Disclosure agreement — After the Federal Court is seized of an application made under paragraph (2)(c) or, in the case of an appeal from, or a review of, an order of the judge made under any of subsections 38.06(1) to (3) in connection with that application, before the appeal or review is disposed of,

(a) the Attorney General of Canada and the person who made the application may enter into an agreement that permits the disclosure of part of the facts referred to in paragraphs 38.02(1)(b) to (d) or part of the information or disclosure of the facts or information subject to conditions; and

(b) if an agreement is entered into, the Court's consideration of the application or any hearing, review or appeal shall be terminated.

(7) Termination of Court consideration, hearing, review or appeal — Subject to subsection (6), after the Federal Court is seized of an application made under this section or, in the case of an appeal from, or a review of, an order of the judge made under any of subsections 38.06(1) to (3), before the appeal or review is disposed of, if the Attorney General of Canada authorizes the disclosure of all or part of the information or withdraws conditions to which the disclosure is subject, the Court's consideration of the application or any hearing, appeal or review shall be terminated in relation to that information, to the extent of the authorization or the withdrawal.

2001, c. 41, ss. 43, 141(7)

38.05 Report relating to proceedings — If he or she receives notice of a hearing under paragraph 38.04(5)(c), a person presiding or designated to preside at the proceeding to which the information relates or, if no person is designated, the person who has the authority to designate a person to preside may, within 10 days after the day on which he or she receives the notice, provide the judge with a report concerning any matter relating to the proceeding that the person considers may be of assistance to the judge.

2001, c. 41, s. 43

38.06 (1) Disclosure order — Unless the judge concludes that the disclosure of the information would be injurious to international relations or national defence or national security, the judge may, by order, authorize the disclosure of the information.

(2) Disclosure order — If the judge concludes that the disclosure of the information would be injurious to international relations or national defence or national security but that the public interest in disclosure outweighs in importance the public interest in non-disclosure, the judge may by order, after considering both the public interest in disclosure and the form of and conditions to disclosure that are most likely to limit any injury to international relations or national defence or national security resulting from disclosure, authorize the disclosure, subject to any conditions that the judge considers appropriate, of all of the information, a part or summary of the information, or a written admission of facts relating to the information.

(3) Order confirming prohibition — If the judge does not authorize disclosure under subsection (1) or (2), the judge shall, by order, confirm the prohibition of disclosure.

(3.1) Evidence — The judge may receive into evidence anything that, in the opinion of the judge, is reliable and appropriate, even if it would not otherwise be admissible under Canadian law, and may base his or her decision on that evidence.

(4) Introduction into evidence — A person who wishes to introduce into evidence material the disclosure of which is authorized under subsection (2) but who may not be able to do so in a proceeding by reason of the rules of admissibility that apply in the proceeding may request from a judge an order permitting the introduction into evidence of the material in a form or subject to any conditions fixed by that judge, as long as that form and those conditions comply with the order made under subsection (2).

(5) Relevant factors — For the purpose of subsection (4), the judge shall consider all the factors that would be relevant for a determination of admissibility in the proceeding.

2001, c. 41, s. 43

38.07 Notice of order — The judge may order the Attorney General of Canada to give notice of an order made under any of subsections 38.06(1) to (3) to any person who, in the opinion of the judge, should be notified.

2001, c. 41, s. 43

38.08 Automatic review — If the judge determines that a party to the proceeding whose interests are adversely affected by an order made under any of subsections 38.06(1) to (3) was not given the opportunity to make representations under paragraph 38.04(5)(d), the judge shall refer the order to the Federal Court of Appeal for review.

2001, c. 41, s. 43

38.09 (1) Appeal to Federal Court of Appeal — An order made under any of subsections 38.06(1) to (3) may be appealed to the Federal Court of Appeal.

(2) Limitation period for appeal — An appeal shall be brought within 10 days after the day on which the rder is made or within any further time that the Court considers appropriate in he circumstances.

2001, c. 41, 43

38.1 Limitation periods for appeals to Supreme Court of Canada — Notwithstanding any other Act of Parliament,

(a) an application for leave to appeal to the Supreme Court of Canada from a judgment made on appeal shall be made within 10 days after the day on which the judgment appealed from is made or within any further time that the Supreme Court of Canada considers appropriate in the circumstances; and
(b) if leave to appeal is granted, the appeal shall be brought in the manner set out in subsection 60(1) of the *Supreme Court Act* but within the time specified by the Supreme Court of Canada.

2001, c. 41, s. 43

38.11 (1) Special rules — A hearing under subsection 38.04(5) or an appeal or review of an order made under any of subsections 38.06(1) to (3) shall be heard in private and, at the request of either the Attorney General of Canada or, in the case of a proceeding under Part III of the *National Defence Act*, the Minister of National Defence, shall be heard in the National Capital Region, as described in the schedule to the *National Capital Act*.

(2) Ex *parte* representations — The judge conducting a hearing under subsection 38.04(5) or the court hearing an appeal or review of an order made under any of subsections 38.06(1) to (3) may give any person who makes representations under paragraph 38.04(5)(d), and shall give the Attorney General of Canada and, in the case of a proceeding under Part III of the *National Defence Act,* the Minister of National Defence, the opportunity to make representations ex parte.

2001, c. 41, s. 43

38.12 (1) Protective order — The judge conducting a hearing under subsection 38.04(5) or the court hearing an appeal or review of an order made under any of subsections 38.06(1) to (3) may make any order that the judge or the court considers appropriate in the circumstances to protect the confidentiality of the information to which the hearing, appeal or review relates.

(2) Court records — The court records relating to the hearing, appeal or review are confidential. The judge or the court may order that the records be sealed and kept in a location to which the public has no access.

2001, c. 41, s. 43

38.13 (1) Certificate of Attorney General of Canada — The Attorney General of Canada may personally issue a certificate that prohibits the disclosure of information in connection with a proceeding for the purpose of protecting information obtained in confidence from, or in relation to, a foreign entity as defined in subsection 2(1) of the Security of Information Act or for the purpose of protecting national defence or national security. The certificate may only be issued after an order or decision that would result in the disclosure of the information to be subject to the certificate has been made under this or any other Act of Parliament.

(2) Military proceedings — In the case of a proceeding under Part III of the *National Defence Act,* the Attorney General of Canada may issue the certificate only with the agreement, given personally, of the Minister of National Defence.

(3) Service of certificate — The Attorney General of Canada shall cause a copy of the certificate to be served on

(a) the person presiding or designated to preside at the proceeding to which the information relates or, if no person is designated, the person who has the authority to designate a person to preside;

(b) every party to the proceeding;

(c) every person who gives notice under section 38.01 in connection with the proceeding;

(d) every person who, in connection with the proceeding, may disclose, is required to disclose or may cause the disclosure of the information about which the Attorney General of Canada has received notice under section 38.01;

(e) every party to a hearing under subsection 38.04(5) or to an appeal of an order made under any of subsections 38.06(1) to (3) in relation to the information;

(f) the judge who conducts a hearing under subsection 38.04(5) and any court that hears an appeal from, or review of, an order made under any of subsections 38.06(1) to (3) in relation to the information; and

(g) any other person who, in the opinion of the Attorney General of Canada, should be served.

(4) Filing of certificate — The Attorney General of Canada shall cause a copy of the certificate to be filed

(a) with the person responsible for the records of the proceeding to which the information relates; and

(b) in the Registry of the Federal Court and the registry of any court that hears an appeal from, or review of, an order made under any of subsections 38.06(1) to (3).

(5) Effect of certificate — If the Attorney General of Canada issues a certificate, then, notwithstanding any other provision of this Act, disclosure of the information shall be prohibited in accordance with the terms of the certificate.

(6) Statutory Instruments Act does not apply — The *Statutory Instruments Act* does not apply to a certificate issued under subsection (1).

(7) Publication — The Attorney General of Canada shall, without delay after a certificate is issued, cause the certificate to be published in the Canada Gazette.

(8) Restriction — The certificate and any matters arising out of it are not subject to review or to be restrained, prohibited, removed, set aside or otherwise dealt with, except in accordance with section 38.131.

(9) Expiration — The certificate expires 15 years after the day on which it is issued and may be reissued.

2001, c. 41, s. 43

38.131 (1) Application for review of certificate — A party to the proceeding referred to in section 38.13 may apply to the Federal Court of Appeal for an order varying or cancelling a certificate issued under that section on the grounds referred to in subsection (8) or (9), as the case may be.

(2) Notice to Attorney General of Canada — The applicant shall give notice of the application to the Attorney General of Canada.

(3) Military proceedings — In the case of proceedings under Part III of the *National Defence Act*, notice under subsection (2) shall be given to both the Attorney General of Canada and the Minister of National Defence.

(4) Single judge — Notwithstanding section 16 of the *Federal Court Act*, for the purposes of the application, the Federal Court of Appeal consists of a single judge of that Court.

(5) Admissible information — In considering the application, the judge may receive into evidence anything that, in the opinion of the judge, is reliable and appropriate, even if it would not otherwise be admissible under Canadian law, and may base a determination made under any of subsections (8) to (10) on that evidence.

(6) Special rules and protective order — Sections 38.11 and 38.12 apply, with any necessary modifications, to an application made under subsection (1).

(7) Expedited consideration — The judge shall consider the application as soon as reasonably possible, but not later than 10 days after the application is made under subsection (1).

(8) Varying the certificate — If the judge determines that some of the information subject to the certificate does not relate either to information obtained in confidence from, or in relation to, a foreign entity as defined in subsection 2(1) of the *Security of Information Act*, or to national defence or national security, the judge shall make an order varying the certificate accordingly.

(9) Cancelling the certificate — If the judge determines that none of the information subject to the certificate relates to information obtained in confidence from, or in relation to, a foreign entity as defined in subsection 2(1) of the *Security of Information Act*, or to national defence or national security, the judge shall make an order cancelling the certificate.

(10) Confirming the certificate — If the judge determines that all of the information subject to the certificate relates to information obtained in confidence from, or in relation to, a foreign entity as defined in subsection 2(1) of the *Security of Information Act*, or to national defence or national security, the judge shall make an order confirming the certificate.

(11) Determination is final — Notwithstanding any other Act of Parliament, a determination of a judge under any of subsections (8) to (10) is final and is not subject to review or appeal by any court.

(12) Publication — If a certificate is varied or cancelled under this section, the Attorney General of Canada shall, as soon as possible after the decision of the judge and in a manner that mentions the original publication of the certificate, cause to be published in the Canada Gazette

(a) the certificate as varied under subsection (8); or
(b) a notice of the cancellation of the certificate under subsection (9).

2001, c. 41, s. 43; 2004, c. 12, s. 19

38.14 (1) Protection of right to a fair trial — The person presiding at a criminal proceeding may make any order that he or she considers appropriate in the circumstances to protect the right of the accused to a fair trial, as long as that order complies with the terms of any order made under any of subsections 38.06(1) to (3) in relation to that proceeding, any judgment made on appeal from, or review of, the order, or any certificate issued under section 38.13.

(2) Potential orders — The orders that may be made under subsection (1) include, but are not limited to, the following orders:

(a) an order dismissing specified counts of the indictment or information, or permitting the indictment or information to proceed only in respect of a lesser or included offence;
(b) an order effecting a stay of the proceedings; and
(c) an order finding against any party on any issue relating to information the disclosure of which is prohibited.

2001, c. 41, s. 43

38.15 (1) Fiat — If sensitive information or potentially injurious information may be disclosed in connection with a prosecution that is not instituted by the Attorney General of Canada or on his or her behalf, the

Attorney General of Canada may issue a fiat and serve the fiat on the prosecutor.

(2) Effect of fiat — When a fiat is served on a prosecutor, the fiat establishes the exclusive authority of the Attorney General of Canada with respect to the conduct of the prosecution described in the fiat or any related process.

(3) Fiat filed in court — If a prosecution described in the fiat or any related process is conducted by or on behalf of the Attorney General of Canada, the fiat or a copy of the fiat shall be filed with the court in which the prosecution or process is conducted.

(4) Fiat constitutes conclusive proof — The fiat or a copy of the fiat

(a) is conclusive proof that the prosecution described in the fiat or any related process may be conducted by or on behalf of the Attorney General of Canada; and

(b) is admissible in evidence without proof of the signature or official character of the Attorney General of Canada.

(5) Military proceedings — This section does not apply to a proceeding under Part III of the *National Defence Act*.

2001, c. 41, s. 43

38.16 Regulations — The Governor in Council may make any regulations that the Governor in Council considers necessary to carry into effect the purposes and provisions of sections 38 to 38.15, including regulations respecting the notices, certificates and the fiat.

2001, c. 41, s. 43

Confidences of the Queen's Privy Council for Canada

[Heading added 2001, c. 41, s. 43.]

39. (1) Objection relating to a confidence of the Queen's Privy Council — Where a minister of the Crown or the Clerk of the Privy Council objects to the disclosure of information before a court, person or body with jurisdiction to compel the production of information by certifying in writing that the information constitutes a confidence of the

Queen's Privy Council for Canada, disclosure of the information shall be refused without examination or hearing of the information by the court, person or body.

(2) Definition — For the purpose of subsection (1), "a confidence of the Queen's Privy Council for Canada" includes, without restricting the generality thereof, information contained in

(a) a memorandum the purpose of which is to present proposals or recommendations to Council;

(b) a discussion paper the purpose of which is to present background explanations, analyses of problems or policy options to Council for consideration by Council in making decisions;

(c) an agendum of Council or a record recording deliberations or decisions of Council;

(d) a record used for or reflecting communications or discussions between ministers of the Crown on matters relating to the making of government decisions or the formulation of government policy;

(e) a record the purpose of which is to brief ministers of the Crown in relation to matters that are brought before, or are proposed to be brought before, Council or that are the subject of communications or discussions referred to in paragraph (d); and

(f) draft legislation.

(3) Definition of "council" — For the purposes of subsection (2), "Council" means the Queen's Privy Council for Canada, committees of the Queen's Privy Council for Canada, Cabinet and committees of Cabinet.

(4) Exception — Subsection (1) does not apply in respect of

(a) a confidence of the Queen's Privy Council for Canada that has been in existence for more than twenty years; or

(b) a discussion paper described in paragraph (2)(b)

(i) if the decisions to which the discussion paper relates have been made public, or

(ii) where the decisions have not been made public, if four years have passed since the decisions were made.

Provincial Laws of Evidence

40. How applicable — In all proceedings over which Parliament has legislative authority, the laws of evidence in force in the province in which those proceedings are taken, including the laws of proof of service of any warrant, summons, subpoena or other document, subject to this Act and other Acts of Parliament, apply to those proceedings.

Statutory Declarations

41. Solemn declaration — Any judge, notary public, justice of the peace, provincial court judge, recorder, mayor or commissioner authorized to take affidavits to be used either in the provincial or federal courts, or any other functionary authorized by law to administer an oath in any matter, may receive the solemn declaration of any person voluntarily making the declaration before him, in the following form, in attestation of the execution of any writing, deed or instrument, or of the truth of any fact, or of any account rendered in writing:

I, ..., solemnly declare that (*state the fact or facts declared to*), and I make this solemn declaration conscientiously believing it to be true, and knowing that it is of the same force and effect as if made under oath. Declared before me ..... at ..... this ..... day of ..... 19 ...

R.S.C. 1985, c. 27 (1st Supp.), s. 203

Insurance Proofs

42. Affidavits, etc — Any affidavit, solemn affirmation or declaration required by any insurance company authorized by law to do business in Canada, in regard to any loss of or injury to person, property or life insured or assured therein, may be taken before any commissioner or other person authorized to take affidavits, before any justice of the peace or before any notary public for any province, and the commissioner, person, justice of the peace or notary public is required to take the affidavit, solemn affirmation or declaration.

PART II

Application

43. Foreign courts — This Part applies to the taking of evidence relating to proceedings in courts out of Canada.

Interpretation

44. Definitions — In this Part,

"cause" includes a proceeding against a criminal;

"court" means any superior court in any province;

"judge" means any judge of any superior court in any province;

"oath" includes a solemn affirmation in cases in which, by the law of Canada, or of a province, as the case may be, a solemn affirmation is allowed instead of an oath.

45. Construction — This Part shall not be so construed as to interfere with the right of legislation of the legislature of any province requisite or desirable for the carrying out of the objects hereof.

Procedure

46. (1) Order for examination of witness in Canada — If, on an application for that purpose, it is made to appear to any court or judge that any court or tribunal outside Canada, before which any civil, commercial or criminal matter is pending, is desirous of obtaining the testimony in relation to that matter of a party or witness within the jurisdiction of the first mentioned court, of the court to which the judge belongs or of the judge, the court or judge may, in its or their discretion, order the examination on oath on interrogatories, or otherwise, before any person or persons named in the order, of that party or witness accordingly, and by the same or any subsequent order may command the attendance of that party or witness for the purpose of being examined, and for the production of any writings or other documents mentioned in the order and of any other writings or documents relating to the matter in question that are in the possession or power of that party or witness.

(2) Video links, etc. — For greater certainty, testimony for the purposes of subsection (1) may be given by means of technology that permits the virtual presence of the party or witness before the court or tribunal outside Canada or that permits that court or tribunal, and the parties, to hear and examine the party or witness.

1999, c. 18, s. 89

47. Enforcement of the order — On the service on the party or witness of an order referred to in section 46, and of an appointment of a time and place for the examination of the party or witness signed by the person named in the order for taking the examination, or, if more than one person is named, by one of the persons named, and on payment or tender of the like conduct money as is properly payable on attendance at a trial, the order may be enforced in like manner as an order made by the court or judge in a cause pending in that court or before that judge.

48. Expenses and conduct money — Every person whose attendance is required in manner described in section 47 is entitled to the like conduct money and payment for expenses and loss of time as on attendance at a trial.

49. Administering oath — On any examination of parties or witnesses, under the authority of any order made in pursuance of this Part, the oath shall be administered by the person authorized to take the examination, or, if more than one person is authorized, by one of those persons.

50. (1) Right of refusal to answer or produce document — Any person examined under any order made under this Part has the like right to refuse to answer questions tending to criminate himself, or other questions, as a party or witness, as the case may be, would have in any cause pending in the court by which, or by a judge whereof, the order is made.

(1.1) Laws about witnesses to apply — video links etc. — Despite subsection (1), when a party or witness gives evidence under subsection 46(2), the evidence shall be given as though they were physically before the court or tribunal outside Canada, for the purposes of the laws relating to evidence and procedure but only to the extent that giving the evidence would not disclose information otherwise protected by the Canadian law of non-disclosure of information or privilege.

(1.2) Contempt of court in Canada — When a party or witness gives evidence under subsection 46(2), the Canadian law relating to contempt of court applies with respect to a refusal by the party or witness to answer a question or to produce a writing or document referred to in subsection 46(1), as ordered under that subsection by the court or judge.

(2) Nature of right — No person shall be compelled to produce, under any order referred to in subsection (1), any writing or other document that he could not be compelled to produce at a trial of such a cause.

1999, c. 18, s. 90

51. (1) Rules of court — The court may frame rules and orders in relation to procedure and to the evidence to be produced in support of the application for an order for examination of parties and witnesses under this Part, and generally for carrying this Part into effect.

(2) Letters rogatory — In the absence of any order in relation to the evidence to be produced in support of the application referred to in subsection (1), letters rogatory from a court or tribunal outside Canada in which the civil, commercial or criminal matter is pending, are deemed and taken to be sufficient evidence in support of the application.

1999, c. 18, s. 91

PART III

Application

52. Application of this Part — This Part extends to the following classes of persons:

(a) officers of any of Her Majesty's diplomatic or consular services while performing their functions in any foreign country, including ambassadors, envoys, ministers, charges d'affaires, counsellors, secretaries, attaches, consuls general, consuls, vice-consuls, pro-consuls, consular agents, acting consuls general, acting consuls, acting vice-consuls and acting consular agents;

(b) officers of the Canadian diplomatic, consular and representative services while performing their functions in any foreign country or in any part of the Commonwealth and Dependent Territories other than Canada, including, in addition to the diplomatic and consular officers mentioned in paragraph (a), high commissioners, permanent delegates, acting high commissioners, acting permanent delegates, counsellors and secretaries;

(c) Canadian Government Trade Commissioners and Assistant Canadian Government Trade Commissioners while performing their functions in any foreign country or in any part of the Commonwealth and Dependent Territories other than Canada;

(d) honorary consular officers of Canada while performing their functions in any foreign country or in any part of the Commonwealth and Dependent Territories other than Canada;

(e) judicial officials in a foreign country in respect of oaths, affidavits, solemn affirmations, declarations or similar documents that the official is authorized to administer, take or receive; and

(f) persons locally engaged and designated by the Deputy Minister of Foreign Affairs or any other persons authorized by that Deputy Minister while performing their functions in any foreign country or in any part of the Commonwealth and Dependent Territories other than Canada.

1994, c. 44, s. 92; 1997, c. 18, s. 118

Oaths and Solemn Affirmations

53. Oaths taken abroad — Oaths, affidavits, solemn affirmations or declarations administered, taken or received outside Canada by any person mentioned in section 52, are as valid and effectual and are of the like force and effect to all intents and purposes as if they had been administered, taken or received in Canada by a person authorized to administer, take or receive oaths, affidavits, solemn affirmations or declarations therein that are valid and effectual under this Act.

Documentary Evidence

54. (1) Documents to be admitted in evidence — Any document that purports to have affixed, impressed or subscribed on it or to it the signature of any person authorized by any of paragraphs 52 (a) to (d) to administer, take or receive oaths, affidavits, solemn affirmations or declarations, together with their seal or with the seal or stamp of their office, or the office to which the person is attached, in testimony of any oath, affidavit, solemn affirmation or declaration being administered, taken or received by the person, shall be admitted in evidence, without proof of the seal or stamp or of the person's signature or official character.

(2) Status of statements — An affidavit, solemn affirmation, declaration or other similar statement taken or received in a foreign country by an official referred to in paragraph 52(e) shall be admitted in evidence without proof of the signature or official character of the official appearing to have signed the affidavit, solemn affirmation, declaration or other statement.

1994, c. 44, s. 93

INDEX